THANK
Rosendale

NEW YORK - THE EMPIRE STATE

Peter P. Genero

Published by:

1904 York Court
Fort Pierce, FL 34982

E-Mail: ppgenero@aol.com

Printed in the United States of America

Library of Congress-in-Publication Data

Genero, Peter P.
THANK ROSENDALE: New York - The Empire State/Peter P.
Genero

1. Title, 2. History- 3. Economic Development, 4. Industrial
Development
TXu001 - 209 - 269

ISBN: 0-9759419-1-7

Cover , New York City, Circa 1884, Currier & Ives
Courtesy Library of Congress

TABLE OF CONTENTS

PROLOGUE 1

INTRODUCTION 3

CHAPTER I   ROSENDALE TODAY 5

CHAPTER II   ROSENDALE – THE BEGINNING 13

CHAPTER III   ROSENDALE – COLONIAL TIMES 23

CHAPTER IV   ROSENDALE CEMENT 30

CHAPTER V   COAL 42

CHAPTER VI   CANALS 49

CHAPTER VII   CANALS-USA 55

CHAPTER VIII   DELAWARE & HUDSON CANAL – PHASE I 64

CHAPTER IX   DELAWARE & HUDSON CANAL – PHASE II 74

CHAPTER X   ROSENDALE – 19TH CENTURY 84

CHAPTER XI   THE WATER WHEEL 95

CHAPTER XII   STEAM POWER – PHASE I 105

CHAPTER XIII   STEAM POWER – PHASE II 116

CHAPTER XIV   INDUSTRIAL DEVELOPMENT – GENERAL 127

CHAPTER XV   INDUSTRIAL DEVELOPMENT – USA 135

CHAPTER XVI   INDUSTRIAL DEVELOPMENT – NEW YORK 143

CHAPTER XVII   ALTERNATIVE SUPPLIERS OF COAL 155

CHAPTER XVIII   THANK ROSENDALE 164

REFLECTIONS 168

ACKNOWLEDGMENTS 169

BIBLIOGRAPHY 171

INDEX 175

ILLUSTRATIONS

Map of New York 6

Cement Vertical Kiln, Rosendale, NY 35

Cooperage 38

Lawrenceville Cement Company, Rosendale, NY 40

Map of Major Canals New York 61

Map of Delaware & Hudson Canal 73

New York Cement Company, Rosendale, NY 78

Stockpile of Coal, Honesdale, PA 79

Lock #7, Rosendale, Delaware & Hudson Canal 82

Joppenberg Mountain (before), Rosendale, NY 92

Joppenberg Mountain (after), Rosendale, NY 92

Newcomen Steam Engine 106

Newcomen Steam Engine, Henry Ford Museum 107

Watt Steam Engine 109

Robert Fulton's Clermont 112

Evans Steam Engine 118

Stockpiles of Coal, Rondout/Kingston, NY 147

Map of Alternative Canal/Coal Routes 156

This book is dedicated to my parents,
Peter Genero and Mary Stjepovich Genero, who worked
their entire adult lives in Rosendale.
At the time of his death, Peter Genero was the senior
kiln burner for the Century Cement Company, home of
the Brooklyn Bridge cement.

PROLOGUE

During World War II in the South Pacific, the author shared a tent with John Links, a professor of English literature from Ohio. John was asked, "What makes a good book?" He replied, "Writing something new," or "Writing something old in a better manner." It is hoped that this book falls into the first category.

It is intended that *Thank Rosendale* be both succinct and readable. During research, many scholarly and thoroughly documented sources were examined. They were well written, but lengthy and dull. One book had 52 pages of footnotes and 845 specific references. If the reader can be informed in a less tedious manner of a new perspective concerning the industrial revolution, which took place in New York during the 19th Century, then this book will have served its purpose.

INTRODUCTION

The cover of this book depicts the harbor of New York City including the Brooklyn Bridge that engineering marvel of the century. It was sketched by Currier & Ives, as seen from the Statue of Liberty shortly after its completion in 1883. It reflects the unprecedented industrial and commercial development that took place, not only in the city, but in the entire state during the 19th Century. The purpose of this book is to establish the fact that we should *Thank Rosendale*, not only for its role in building the Brooklyn Bridge and locating the Statue of Liberty in New York's harbor, but most importantly, for New York becoming the "Empire State" of the nation.

It all began in the 19th Century with the discovery of "gray gold" in Rosendale. This started a chain reaction of events, which led to the unbelievable industrial revolution taking place in the state at that time. In some respects, it was similar to that old adage, "For want of a nail, a shoe was lost; for want of a shoe, a horse went lame, etc.", until an entire kingdom was lost. As with the adage, this discovery initiated a number of events, culminating with New York taking over the lead in the nation's industrial growth and becoming the "Empire State." Had this discovery not taken place, it is quite certain that the Statue of Liberty would not have been placed in New York, the building of the Brooklyn Bridge would have been delayed until the next century, and New York's industrial growth would have been sharply curtailed.

There are some who will not accept the concept that Rosendale was the cornerstone upon which the industrial development of New York was built. Generally, they believe that the Erie Canal fulfilled that role. There is no wish to negate the importance of the Erie Canal in the economic development of the state. The Erie Canal was important, very important, and much credit is given to it in this book. However, with the Erie Canal alone, the economic development of New York would have taken a different path. It would have continued on its way of becoming only a mercantile center for the buying, selling, and trading of goods and services. As such, it would have had fierce competition from other mercantile centers such as Boston and Philadelphia, with possibly a different outcome. Also, by the time of the Civil War, the nation had many canals, over 4,000 miles of them. Relying on the Erie Canal alone, New York would not have emerged as the industrial giant that it later became.

There are others who point to the building of railroads as the key factor in the industrial development of New York. It is true that they were an important factor in the industrial development of the nation, but they were equally available to almost all of the other states as well. Railroads were a little late arriving on the scene, and New York would not have gained any significant or unique advantage from them over the other states. Further, it is an historical fact that once the railroads were in place as the dominate means of transportation, industrial development moved westward. It might also be mentioned that from an industrial development viewpoint, it was still cheaper to ship many bulk items, such as coal, via canals until almost the end of the 19th Century.

As for the electrical age, it too was late arriving on the scene. Its major impact took place during the 20th Century. Also, it was equally available to other states, with no major special benefits to the State of New York.

Briefly stated, it was Rosendale (the D&H Canal, Rosendale cement, the steam engine, and coal) which made the difference. Therefore, one can state quite correctly, that for whatever New York is today, good or bad, *Thank Rosendale.*

CHAPTER I

ROSENDALE – TODAY

Rosendale today is a peaceful and attractive community with a population of about 5,000, located about 100 miles north of Times Square, New York City. It is in the foothills of the Catskill Mountains and just a few miles west of the Hudson River.

Although the New York Thruway (I-87) goes through the township, the highway builders did not see fit to have an exit for Rosendale. One must use the exit at Kingston, 8 miles north, or the exit at New Paltz, 8 miles south. This is a blessing in disguise, since it contributes greatly to the tranquility and quality of life in the area.

There are no factories or industries in Rosendale. The two major business enterprises are Williams Lake, a classic old-fashioned Catskill Mountain resort, and Hidden Valley, an attractive picnicking and camping ground. As a result, Rosendale has become a bedroom community for the cities of Kingston and New Paltz. Also, many of the residents are senior citizens and retirees from New York City. There are even a few hardy souls who still work in the New York metropolitan area and commute back and forth by bus and auto. Despite this laid-back atmosphere, the last few years have seen Rosendale develop into quite an artist colony. It has not yet gained the renown of Woodstock, but it is slowly gaining ground.

Meandering through the area flows the Rondout Creek, perfect for picnicking, fishing, and, in by-gone years, for swimming. The numerous natural swimming holes are still around, but sadly, lightly used. It seems that today's youth prefer chlorinated swimming pools, with refreshment stands, lifeguards, and all sorts of safety rules and regulations.

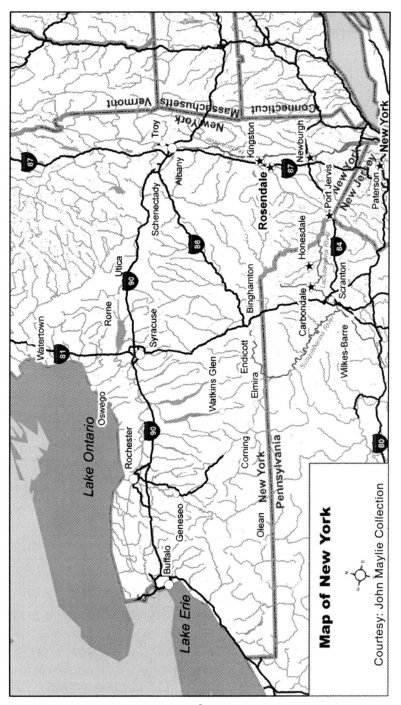

Map of New York

Courtesy: John Maylie Collection

Admittedly, the Rondout Creek is not as full or free flowing as in years past when there were sluiceways every few miles to turn water wheels. These, in turn, powered grist mills, saw mills, and work shops along its route. This continued until the early 20th Century when politics and the needs of others entered the scene. The powerful political forces of New York City convinced the state authorities to divert some of this pristine water to their use. The watershed of the Rondout Creek and other water resources of the southern Catskill Mountains were chosen to fill this need. The creek still flows with grace and beauty through the valley, but with somewhat less force.

All is not lost however, for the younger generation has arrived to make appropriate use of this still attractive natural resource. Due to its natural environment, the level of the water in the creek will rise quickly after moderate and heavy rains. A rise of 2 to 10 feet, lasting several days, is not uncommon. As a result, Rosendale has become a center for "kayaking." After every significant rainfall, the creek becomes a beehive of activity. Usually, the boaters launch their kayaks below the dam at High Falls, about 10 miles from the Hudson River. Then they paddle, or simply steer, since the current is so swift, all the way to the Hudson River. They go over the rapids in Lawrenceville, through the sluiceway of the no longer existing grist-mill, under the ancient Walkill Valley railroad bridge, past the old Village of Rosendale, through the treacherous waters of LeFever Falls and on to the placid waters of the Rondout/Walkill estuary at Eddyville. Finally, they can go past Kingston/Rondout into the Hudson River and as far north or south as they desire.

Wildlife is also abundant in the area. It is a veritable bird-watcher's paradise and a nature lover's delight. Birds abound, from the smallest humming bird to the largest of ducks, geese, swans, and herons. Raccoons, squirrels, chipmunks, rabbits, woodchucks, muskrats, large turtles, and even an occasional bear wander up and down the creek. Deer are particularly plentiful. One local family insists that for the last fifty years, they have bagged a deer each year and never had to travel more than a mile from their house, which is located in the center of old Rosendale. For those interested in reptiles, they too will find a great variety. Most are harmless, but there are also occasional copperheads and rattlers. For those interested in fresh water fishing, the creek thrives with bass, chub, sunfish, etc. The creek has a plentiful supply of the rare dobson, the best live fish bait for the serious angler.

Other than the contents of this book, Rosendale has only two other claims to fame of historical note. First, George Washington's Continental Army once encamped there. It seems that after the Declaration of Independence, New York revolutionaries assembled and declared New York an independent state with Kingston as its capital. On October 3, 1777, the British, under the command of Sir Henry Clinton, captured and burned Kingston. The assembly fled to nearby Hurley. This was during the disastrous British campaign to gain control of the Hudson River, Albany, and Lake Champlain, thereby cutting the rebellious colonies in half. The Continental Army, under the command of General/Governor George Clinton, marched north from West Point in an effort to save the city (Clinton versus Clinton). George Washington was busy trying to protect Philadelphia. The army crossed the Rondout Creek by means of a ford in the old Village of Rosendale. However, it was discovered that the city of Kingston was already in flames. Realizing that it was too late to save the city, the army spent the night in Rosendale and returned to West Point the next day.

The second, and probably Rosendale's more widely known claim to fame, is that it was long considered to be the birthplace of Sojourner Truth. She was a slave and since no official records of slaves were kept at that time, the exact date and place of her birth are difficult to verify. Evidently, she was born before 1800 on a farm once owned by Jacob Rusten,

Rosendale's first settler. The nearby town of Esopus now claims the honor and has erected a plaque commemorating the event.

After being bought, sold, auctioned, and traded a number of times, she was finally given her freedom about 1827, after New York's anti-slavery laws became fully effective. She lived for about one hundred years and became a reknowned black leader, author, lecturer, and evangelist. Not knowing how to read or write, she dictated her works. She promoted women's suffrage and the resettlement of freed slaves. Sojourner Truth was so dynamic and respected that President Lincoln called on her for advice.

Probably, the most prominent landmark in Rosendale today is the ancient iron and steel railroad bridge of the defunct Walkill Valley Railroad. It is about 130 years old and rises about 130 feet above the Rondout Creek. A Mr. John Rahl purchased a good deal of the bankrupt Walkill Valley Railroad, along with its tracks, station houses, bridges, and roadways. He turned the bridge into one of the most popular tourist attractions in the area. The view from it is outstanding, especially during the fall. The colors of the leaves on the surrounding hills are remarkable. They will challenge any of the more touted tourist sites, even those along the famed Appalachian Trail.

In recent times, the bridge has been used for many purposes, some pleasant and some not so pleasant. The old bridge is popular for picnics, barbecues, and especially for artists and photographers. Some have tried bungee jumping from it, one without a restraining cord. At least one couple was married on the bridge. In the future, some may find more innovative uses for the old bridge, but whatever the use, it will always be one of the best places from which to drink in the natural beauty of the Rondout Creek Valley.

Rosendale is really the type of small town that we read about, hear about, and even imagine. It is the kind of town that Thorton Wilder must have had in mind when he wrote his famous play, *Our Town*. The old Village of Rosendale is so un-prepossessing that recently it decided to discontinue itself as an independent political entity. It merged itself into the Township of Rosendale. Sadly there will no longer be a "Mayor of Rosendale."

As explained in Chapter X, the Township of Rosendale was established in the 19th Century to unite the cement mining communities. It performs the usual local government functions such as trash collection, local road repair, water and sewer services, fire/rescue, police protection, etc. The three man police force is not unlike that of Andy Griffith's Mayberry. The fire/rescue force is on a volunteer basis. When the siren sounds, the volunteers drop whatever they are doing and rush to where they are needed. Interestingly, the fire/rescue units have unique ways of financing their needs. Each year, one of the units will park its engine along the main road and hold out an empty fireman's boot to collect donations from the passing motorists. Another, will hold a giant "all you can eat" banquet with the food and refreshments supplied by the families of the volunteers. There is no end to their community spirit.

Public education has changed dramatically. Rosendale has now joined its counterparts around the nation. Earlier, there were six one-room school houses and one two-room school house. These were scattered throughout the township, and all of the children (including the author) walked to school. Now, there is one gigantic centralized school district with an enormous budget, many buildings, buses, teachers, and counselors.

All in all, there is still much community spirit, and the residents still hold a number of public events and public ceremonies. One of the most heart warming takes place on Memorial Day. Each year, they have a Memorial Day parade with a number of local groups participating, some young and some not so young, each trying to do his/her best. The route is about two miles long and passes through the villages of Tilson and Rosendale. The parade terminates at the intersection of the state roads 32 and 213, at the Veteran's Memorial. There honor is paid to those who have fallen in the defense of their country. The most moving moments of all are when the parade passes the two cemeteries along the route of march. At each cemetery, the band halts and faces the gravesites. Then, a lone bugler sounds "taps." It's enough to water the eyes of even the most hard hearted of souls.

For the history buffs and those interested in the evolution of Rosendale during the 19th Century, there are two excellent museums in the vicinity. One is the D&H Canal Museum in High Falls and the other is the Century House in Lawrenceville. The Century House is named after the cement that built the Brooklyn Bridge; the D&H Museum is all about the Delaware and Hudson Canal. Both contain extensive dossiers, records, sketches, prints, photographs, artifacts, and countless items of memorabilia from the 19th Century.

Next to the D& H Museum are the remains of some of the old stone locks of the Delaware & Hudson Canal. Also nearby are some of the abutments of the old D&H suspension aqueduct by which canal boats were floated across the Rondout Creek. It was one of the earliest "suspension" type bridges designed and built by John Roebling. He used this experience to hone his skills concerning suspension bridges to later build the Brooklyn Bridge, the longest suspension bridge in the world at that time.

At the Century House museum and estate, one may even go into one of the old mines used to extract the "gray gold" that made Rosendale famous. One may also inspect some of the vertical kilns that were used to manufacture the actual cement that was used to build the Brooklyn Bridge. In addition, one can visit the historic stone house of A.J. Snyder, the last of the cement barons. He had a daily routine of driving through the old village of Rosendale in his elegant shiny buggy, drawn by a beautiful, excellently groomed, gaited mare. He kept up this practice well into the automobile era and almost to the end of his 86 years.

This is Rosendale today. What it was in the past and how it played its momentous role in New York's industrial revolution will be covered in detail in subsequent chapters. Although Rosendale is now virtually forgotten and its character changed, one cannot ignore what has happened in the past. Especially, one cannot forget the pivotal role that it played in charting the future course of the city and state of New York.

Before getting into the details of how Rosendale played such an important role in the development of New York, a cursory review will be made of the early history of the state, starting with Henry Hudson's voyage of discovery.

CHAPTER II

ROSENDALE – THE BEGINNING

Giovanni Verranzano and his crew are generally credited with being the first Europeans to have visited New York. According to his journals, his ship sailed into a harbor resembling New York in 1524. Evidently, they looked around, didn't find anything interesting, and sailed away without making any claims of sovereignty. Verranzano was from Florence, but was sailing under French auspices. Since there were no further attempts to explore the area for almost 100 years, Washington Irving (of Rip Van Winkle fame) considered Verranzano's visit to be only a half-truth.

The next European visitors came to New York in 1609. Their ship was the Half Moon, captained by Henry Hudson. Strangely, he was an Englishman sailing under the Dutch flag. His sailing/navigational skills might be called into question, since he sailed 150 miles up the Hudson River, looking for a short cut to Cathay (China). Unlike Verranzano, he stopped long enough to meet with the natives and explore the possibilities of future trade. The natives were not unfriendly, and Hudson believed that a lucrative trade in furs and hides could be established.

The Dutch East India Company, which sponsored his voyage, was not at all enthusiastic. The company wanted to go to the Far East for gold, silks, and spices. However, this was during the high period of the Dutch reformation and there were others who were always alert for new trading opportunities. A group was formed called the Dutch West Indies Trading Company. Although slow in organizing and financing, it was authorized to conduct all future colonizing and trading activities in New York or New Amsterdam, as it was then called.

By 1614, the Dutch had established Fort Nassau in the Albany area for trading purposes. It was short lived and in 1624, they established Fort Orange on a more permanent basis. This was an area of almost unlimited natural resources. Besides furs and hides, the area was covered entirely with forests. The tall straight pines were especially desired for ships' masts and the oak and other hardwoods were prized for ship building. Fish and game were also plentiful. All in all, maybe they were not as glittering as gold and silks, but they were profitable natural resources, which were needed to replace the dwindling supplies in Europe. At that time, the Dutch claimed what today is New York, New Jersey, Delaware, and part of Connecticut. The interior boundaries were vague.

During the 1624-1626 period, colonization began in earnest. Peter Minuit was appointed the first Director General of New Amsterdam. It was he who bought Manhattan Island for 60 guilders ($24) worth of trinkets and beads, from the Canarse Indians, loosely associated with the Algonquin tribe. He built a fort at the present day Battery Park to protect the settlements. The purchase of Manhattan from the natives established a precedent for the new colonists. Although grants were made from Holland, the natives were always paid for the land on which they lived. This was unlike other colonists, who simply took over land without compensation. The natives of eastern New York, the Catskill Mountains, and the Hudson River Valley were related loosely to the Algonquin Federation. They were less warlike than the Mohawk and Iroquois of western and northern New York. The practice of purchasing the land and the relatively free trading that took place between the natives and the colonists tended to create a "watchful but mostly peaceful" co-existence.

It should be remembered that at this time the natives were in a fairly primitive state of development. The club, lance, bow and arrows with sharpened stones on their tips, were their primary weapons. Any metallic items, such as knives, kettles, pots and pans were unknown to them and much sought after in their trading.

Rum and sugar were equally desirable. The natives, for their part, were very helpful to the colonists. They introduced them to corn, beans, and pumpkins. They also taught them the art of hunting, fishing, and trapping in the New World. The few outbreaks that did occur were usually settled with treaties and an exchange of gifts. There were no attempts to round up the Indians and put them on reservations; that was to come later.

The Dutch hoped that the patroon system would broaden their base of profitability beyond that of fur and lumber. It was quite unique and the effects lasted almost 200 years. It was similar in some respects to the medieval feudal system that was quite prevalent in Europe. A "patroon" was given a grant of land, provided he would bring in 50 tenant farmers to occupy and work the land. Along the Hudson River, the grant was for 16 miles along one side of the river or 8 miles on both sides of the river. If Indians were present, the patroon was expected to pay them for the land. The distance of the grant inland from the river was usually vague. The most successful patroon grant was the one given to Van Rensselaer near Albany. After a few additional purchases from the Indians, his holdings came to about 700,000 acres.

The tenant farmer was expected to clear his own land, build his own house, and pay rent of about 1/10th of his crops to the patroon. In addition, the tenant farmer was expected occasionally to do special chores for the patroon, such as help build a barn and clear a road or a field. Usually, the tenant farmer had the option of buying his farm, and a few did. Most of the tenant farmers were of Dutch, German, or Central European origin. One of the main reasons that the tenant farmers accepted these conditions was that in Europe, besides being landless peasants, they were required to perform harsh military service. At that time, Europe was not only in a constant state of war, but the people had to endure a number of devastating plagues as well.

In the New World, the tenant farmers were expected to serve in the local militia. However, until the French and Indian War, such service was almost a semi-social event. The patroon was expected to maintain a semblance of law and order. He served as a justice of peace, he enforced local laws and, in some instances, his approval had to be obtained before marriage.

The land was bountiful, but equally as important, there was an abundance of fish and game. Although the patroon claimed ownership of all fish and game (similar to the old days of Robin Hood in Sherwood Forest), it was difficult, if not impossible to enforce. The Indians hunted and fished wherever they desired. Who could determine if the farmer caught the fish himself or obtained it from the Indians by trading? Few partoons tried to enforce these rights, but they tried assiduously to do so, insofar as pelts and hides were concerned. Since it was difficult for the tenants to sell them on the open market, the partoon could exercise some control. As a general rule, personal use of these items was not challenged.

During the Dutch period, life in New Amsterdam was not too unpleasant. The Indians did as they pleased. They hunted, fished, raised a few crops, and did a little trading. The tenants continued with their daily tasks and routines. The patroons lived in their manors and the merchants traded with everyone. The Dutch West Indies Company seemed too lazy or corrupt to interfere excessively with local events and with one notable exception – the Director Generals that were appointed managed to hold things together. The one exception, a Willem Kieft, was not above enriching his family and causing the only major open conflict with the local Indians. As a sad case of comeuppance, on his return trip to Holland, he was lost at sea, with all of his ill-gotten gains. There was some whittling away of the colony by the British and Swedes. The last Director General was Peter Stuyvesant, who, despite his wooden leg, did an effective job of keeping the relative peace and keeping the economy flourishing smoothly.

All of this came to an abrupt end in 1664, when a British fleet sailed into New York harbor and demanded its surrender. Peter Stuyvesant wanted to put up a fight, but the merchants and land owners wanted to surrender. The latter were encouraged by the British, who promised that business would continue as usual and that they would honor all existing land titles and grants. On September 8, 1664, Peter Stuyvesant turned over New Amsterdam to Colonel Nicolls, who not only kept his promises, but wisely even retained the practice of paying the Indians for their lands. Colonel Nicolls did make one change. He changed the name from New Amsterdam to New York in honor of his superior in England, the Duke of York.

An interesting historical footnote: The Dutch decided to get even with the British for seizing New Amsterdam. During the winter of 1666-1667, they quietly slipped their fleet out to sea and captured that part of British Guiana known today as Surinam. At the ensuing Treaty of Breda, July 21, 1667, the Dutch conceded New Amsterdam to the British, but demanded and obtained permanent possession of Surinam. At that time, it was generally agreed that the Dutch got the better of the deal. With thousands of slaves from Africa and scores of sugar plantations, the Dutch turned Surinam into one of the pearls of their empire. It might be mentioned that later the Dutch did recapture New York, but held it only briefly.

There was also a so-called "peasants uprising," but in 1691, a new British Royal Governor General arrived and established firm control, which lasted until the American Revolution. The leader of the uprising met the same fate as Captain Kidd.

During the approximate 100 years of British rule, several generalized trends took place, which permitted New York to grow a little differently than the other colonies. Because of the predominately Dutch and German population, the British governed in a more open and tolerant manner. In fact, in Kingston, which was the first capital of New York, Dutch was the dominant language up until and including the revolution. Unlike other colonies, there was wide religious tolerance, with the Dutch Reformed Church being the most popular. This openness tended to attract an ever increasing and wider variety of colonist.

International trade was the primary factor responsible for the growth of the New York harbor area. The Dutch influence predominated and seeking financial profit was placed at the head of all of their endeavors. They were heavily engaged in the infamous "triangular trade." i.e., rum, sugar, and slaves. They were so brazen that they openly sponsored the adventures of not only privateers, but pirates as well.

The term "privateer" is really a misnomer. They were called "privateers" only when the victims were from a country in open conflict with the British. If the victims were not in open conflict with the British, they were most often called "freebooters" or "buccaneers." Only when the victims were British, were they called "pirates." New York, in effect, was a safe haven for all of the above. It was there that their ships were provisioned, repaired, and sometimes even financed. New York was also the place where the booty could be "disposed of" at a profit. Captain Kidd was often a guest in New York. It was there that the British finally captured him and took him to London to be hanged.

Finally, when things got out of hand, the British clamped down and forced the merchants to pursue more legitimate sources of income. This was not too difficult, since New York had good farm land and abounded in natural resources. The tall straight coniferous trees of the Catskills were in great demand worldwide for use as ships' spars and masts. The sales of furs and hides were also very profitable. The manifest of one ship alone listed 7,246 beaver pelts, 853 otter pelts, and 850 other pelts.

Up along the Hudson River and adjacent areas, the population of agriculturally oriented people continued to grow at a modest rate. The British continued the Dutch practice of making grants of land to favored friends and individuals. The most infamous was the Hardenbergh Patent of about 1 1/2 million acres of land. It included the entire Catskill Mountain area from the Hudson River to as far west as one desired. An accurate survey was never made to determine the exact boundaries and to this day, some land titles are still in question. The Rondout Creek in Rosendale was claimed as the southern boundary of the grant. Until recently, the town of Rosendale claimed a park and recreation area from the old Hardenbergh Patent.

In general, the grantee was expected to bring in tenant farmers from Europe, under conditions similar to those of the Dutch Patroon system. The grantee or landlord, lived in his manor, collected rents from his tenants, and engaged in local politics. Unlike the merchants of New York who regarded money as their measure of wealth, the landlords regarded the size of their land holdings as their measure of wealth. As a result, the landlords tried to accumulate as much land as possible. One of the problems that arose out of land ownership was what happened to the land when the owner died. At that time, it was customary to have large families and when the owner died, the land was subdivided among the heirs. It therefore followed that the size of individual holdings became smaller and smaller with each new generation.

It should be mentioned that there were many slaves in New York during this period, as much as 20% of the population around 1700. As the number of tenants and tradesmen from Europe increased, the need for slaves decreased to about 5% at the time of the revolution. Slavery was officially discontinued in 1799, but was not actually ended until 1827.

Population growth was helped by the arrival of whole groups and communities from Europe seeking a better life and the freedom to pursue it in the manner they wished. They were following the examples of the earlier Pilgrims of Plymouth Rock and the Quakers of Pennsylvania. The group that settled in the Rosendale area were the Huguenots, who were fleeing persecution in France. They were industrious farmers and builders, and the town of New Paltz became their center. They farmed the fertile Walkill River Valley, growing grain, fruits and vegetables, as well as producing excellent dairy products. Even today, their apples are considered the pride of New York State. One of their streets in old New Paltz, with its stone houses and flagstone sidewalks, exists today almost exactly as it did almost 250 years ago. It is one of the oldest such streets in the United States.

One unexpected migratory group that helped increase the population of New York was the New England Yankee, mostly from Connecticut and Massachusetts. This tide began in the middle 1700's. One reason was that at home useable land was becoming less plentiful and more expensive. As in New York, when a land owner died, the land was sub-divided among the heirs, and the parcels were becoming smaller and smaller. Also, as members of a family got married, they wanted land of their own, and the available land was becoming more expensive. This was at a time when land just west of Rosendale was selling for as little as fifty cents an acre. Another inducement was the untapped streams and creeks in the Catskill Mountains. Their water power was needed for the grist mills and saw mills, which were requirements for all new settlements.

The preceding is a summary of the development of the Hudson River Valley up until the French and Indian War (1754-1763). During this period, the Rosendale area was relatively tranquil. There were some Indian uprisings, but they were usually settled quickly and on reasonable terms.

Rosendale itself had its origins in a quiet and normal progression of events. Jacob Rusten was an early, successful trader in Kingston. He traveled extensively among the Indians, learned their language, and gained their trust. In the early 1680's, he hired a young assistant from Albany named Johannis Hardenbergh. Together, they made their business thrive. Jacob Rusten became the wealthiest man in Kingston. During this period, he bought from the Indians the fertile Rondout Creek Valley and what is now most of the town of Rosendale. Around 1699, Jacob Rusten turned his business over to Johannis Hardenbergh, who had married his daughter. Jacob Rusten then retired to his manor in Rosendale, becoming its first citizen. He then proceeded to lead a leisurely manor-type life dabbling in local and colonial politics.

Although the name of Rusten is little known outside of Rosendale, Kingston, and New Paltz, his son-in-law, Johannis Hardenbergh became one of the most famous of the early settlers. No history of New York can be written without taking into account the controversial Hardenbergh Patent. Volumes have been written about the intrigue, circumstances, and dealings surrounding this grant. Further, its effects have been the subject of countless litigations for almost three hundred years.

Such was Rosendale about the time of the French and Indian War. Life was not unpleasant. Except for an occasional Indian foray, the entire area enjoyed a period of relative peace and steady economic growth.

The landed gentry, along with the moneyed merchants of the cities, controlled local governmental activities under a governor-general appointed by the British crown. Control was loose and of a semi-benevolent nature. The governor-generals were reasonably competent and except for the Hardenbergh Patent, did not cause too many problems. The inter-marriage among the major landowners and the more successful merchants had the effect of creating a local aristocracy, which helped administer local events.

This situation continued until the French and Indian War. Its result was a classic case of "winning the war, but losing the peace." The victory had unintended consequences and set the stage for the American Revolution.

CHAPTER III

ROSENDALE – COLONIAL TIMES

Historically, the French and Indian War took place from 1754 to 1763. However, most of the major fighting ceased after the fall of Montreal in 1760.

The war did not cause significant hardship or distress along the Hudson River Valley in New York. Except for the active recruitment of volunteers for the local militia, life continued pretty much as usual. Most of the fighting took place on the frontiers to the North and the West, along the axis of the Great Lakes and Saint Lawrence waterways, all some distance from Rosendale. Also, most of the fighting was done by the thousands of British Regulars, supported by Iroquois Indians and some local militia.

During the period of active warfare, both sides made wide use of Indians. Their services were bought with gifts and promises of much booty. The Iroquois in central New York sided with the British, while most of the other Indians, in the North and west, sided with the French. Sometimes they fought with the regulars, but most of the time they raided, plundered, and took prisoners. Local militias were the principal forces used to fight off these raids. Most of the outlying settlers survived by evacuating to the larger settlements or by simply hiding in the forests during the raids. The Indians seldom remained in the area after a raid and quickly moved on to other challenges. The Algonquin Indians of the Hudson River Valley were mostly neutral and preferred to continue hunting, fishing, and tending their small fields. Also, they continued trading with the settlers pretty much as before. As a result, Rosendale and its environs escaped the ravages of war.

Although the peace treaty was signed in Paris on February 10, 1763, the Indians along the frontier paid it little attention.

The following summer, Chief Pontiac captured almost all of the British forts west of Niagara, except Fort Pitt (Pittsburgh) and Detroit. Even after Chief Pontiac was subdued, sporadic skirmishes and raids continued along the frontier. The fact that the war lasted nine long years and there was very little peace during the ensuing years caused serious problems for the colonists, especially those inland from the coastal areas.

The British were forced to keep large numbers of regular forces in the colonies to maintain a reasonable level of peace. To pay for this, the British government decided that the colonists should pay their "fair share"(?). To do so, all types of taxes and levies were placed upon the colonists. This angered the merchants, landowners, and other leading citizens (taxation without representation). However, what angered most of the independent and small farmers was the infamous Quartering Act. This gave the British military the right to enter any settler's house and demand to be sheltered and fed, in other words, forcibly "quartered" in that individual's house. This caused such long lasting resentment that Amendment III was added to the United State Constitution forbidding the "quartering" of troops in private homes without the owner's consent.

As for the American Revolutionary War, volumes have been written about it, so there is no need to rehash what has already been covered in the greatest of detail. This book will be limited to a few of the lesser publicized situations, which directly or indirectly affected the Rosendale area.

The local tenant farmers were mostly neutral. They would have preferred to have been left alone to continue to farm, hunt, fish and provide for their families. Most of the independent farmers, large landowners, merchants, and traders generally supported the Revolution. As always, there were some exceptions.

The Philipse family, probably the wealthiest in the colonies at that time, remained loyal to the British. Besides having the largest grist mills and being the most eminent traders, they owned all of the land from upper Manhattan to the Tappan Zee, including almost all of the Bronx, Yonkers, and Westchester County. Not much note is taken of them in American history because along with 28,000 other Tories, they sailed into oblivion when the British evacuated New York.

During the Revolution, British spies were very active in the Catskill Mountain area. They convinced many of the tenant farmers that if they remained loyal to Britain, they would be granted free and clear title to their farms and would no longer have to pay rents or do other chores for the big land owners. The spies had some success and a number agreed to support the British. A sizeable band of them (about 100) marched south to join the British in New York City. The route they took was from the Catskill Mountains, through Rosendale and southward along the Shawangunk Mountains, home of Lake Mohonk, a plush vacation resort today. However, lacking adequate food and supplies, they foraged among the farms in the Walkill Valley. This so enraged the French Huguenot farmers, that their militia chased them down and captured these marauding loyalists. The two leaders were hanged in Kingston and the remainder were "given an offer they couldn't refuse." The next day, they all volunteered to join the Continental Army.

During the Revolutionary War, marauding bands of Iroquois Indians made a number of raids as far east as the Catskill Mountains and the Hudson River. They were sponsored by the British at Fort Niagara. They pillaged, plundered, and took prisoners. On one such raid near Kingston, they captured a farmer and his son. The rest of the family was saved by hiding in the nearby forest. The captives were taken to Fort Niagara. After about two years, they escaped. The name of the farmer was Jeremiah Snyder who fathered 13 children and had 98 grandchildren. Almost 100 years later, one A. J. Snyder was the owner of the Century Cement Company, the last active natural cement company in Rosendale.

After the Revolutionary War, things became much as they were before the war. Despite promises to the contrary by both sides, the tenant farmers were not given title to their land and were still tenant farmers. The landlords continued living in their manors, collecting stipends from their tenants, and engaging in endless political activities. Oddly, it was not until the anti-rent riots of 1841 that the laws were changed and tenant farmers finally obtained title to their lands. It should be mentioned that those who served in the Continental Army were given land grants as promised (usually 100 acres). However, most land grants were in the western territories, still under control of the Indians.

Small industries grew up wherever there was a small stream or creek, which could be harnessed for water power. This was a time when there were only two sources of power, other than man or beast: wind power, as in windmill, which had some usage in Pennsylvania, and water power, as in water wheel, which had wide use in New England. Water power was used for grist mills, saw mills, paper mills, and tanneries. The latter was aided greatly by the abundance of hemlock bark in the Catskill Mountains, which was used in curing and tanning leather.

Transportation was a major problem, which is why almost all major cities were located in coastal areas. Trails and an occasional turnpike were primitive and unreliable. At that time, a turnpike usually was a wagon trail from which major obstacles such as fallen trees and large rocks had been removed. At a critical point, a log with spikes was placed across the trail. When a toll was paid, the log was twisted or turned so the spikes would lay flat along the ground. This allowed the horse and wagon to pass over it, hence the name "turnpike."

For New York state, the Hudson River proved to be a boon for the traveler and hauler of freight. It provided a long, deep, navigable waterway towards the interior, the best inland transportation route on the Atlantic coast. As many as a thousand boats, sloops, schooners, and ocean going sailing ships plied up and down the river. One historian estimates that the total was more than on the Thames River in London. At that time, Albany, 150 miles up the Hudson River, was considered a major international seaport.

The farmers around Rosendale raised their crops, cultivated their orchards, and tended their animals. These they sold up and down the Hudson River. Corn, buckwheat, hay, and oats were their major crops and milk, butter and cheese their most profitable products. Chickens and hogs were very popular and horses were also quite important.

The business community favored lumber, furs, and leather products. Strange as it may seem today, fresh water fish was a very important item both for home consumption and trade. During the 19th Century, as much as 4,000,000 pounds of shad were being caught in the Hudson River annually.

This was also the beginning of the ice industry in New York. Tens of thousands of tons of ice were not only used locally, but shipped all over the world, including India. The abundance of thick lumber and enormous quantities of sawdust were essential not only for construction of ice houses, but to insulate the cargo holds of the sailing ships.

Throughout the new nation, major events were taking place, but with little change affecting Rosendale.

> The nation's capital was being established along the
>   Potomac River.
> The Northwest Territories were being opened for
>   settlement.

The New Englanders were establishing a primitive,
> but very solid industrial base along its many streams,
> creeks, and waterways.

In the South, agriculture was growing very rapidly,
> and enormous quantities of cotton were being exported.

International trade was blossoming all along the
> Atlantic Seaboard.

The War of 1812, a defining period in American
> history, took place to determine if the country was
> really viable as an independent nation.

Life in Rosendale changed little. During the War of 1812, the local population preferred to be left alone, in much the same manner as during the Revolutionary War. Of course, there were a significant number of volunteers, especially for their local militia. Their military services left much to be desired and in the end, Canada remained part of the British Empire.

The area epitomized the Jeffersonian concept of what America should be. He pictured the backbone of America being the self-sufficient family farm. They would build their own homes, raise or catch their own food, and make their own clothing and housewares. At one point during his presidency, Jefferson even abolished the national army. He reasoned that if each community had its own militia to defend itself, there was no need for a national army.

The foregoing are snippets of Rosendale life up to the Revolutionary War and for a short period thereafter. The population was about 90% rural. The tenant farmers, independent farmers, landlords, and merchants continued as before the Revolution. Shortly thereafter, Currier and Ives recorded this era for all posterity in their prints and sketches.

According to a New York state historical marker at the intersection of State Road 213 and Bruceville Road in High Falls/Rosendale, an event took place in 1818 which had great consequences. Legend has it that a blacksmith named Nathaniel Bruce was preparing his forge for his daily tasks. He used small chunks of the local limestone to husband the hot coals in his forge. At the end of the day, he noticed that the limestone had turned into a sort of "clinker." Normally, these were discarded. He had heard stories of some strange uses of limestone, including its use as a fertilizer. He ground the clinker into a powder and mixed it with water. The slurry turned into a substance, which was as hard as a rock. It was natural cement.

The discovery of Rosendale cement initiated a sequence of events, which had a monumental impact on the industrial revolution and economic development of the state of New York.

CHAPTER IV

ROSENDALE CEMENT

Cement was the basic reason why Rosendale became the cornerstone for the industrial development of the state of New York. It is important that we understand a little about cement: what it is, its history, how it is produced, and why Rosendale played such an important role in its development.

Today, it is an indisputable fact that cement is the most desired and most widely used construction material in the world. This was not always so. The history of cement is a little unusual, in that it did not come into its current prominence by means of a steady evolutionary process.

In the ancient world, Assyria and Babylonia used a dried and hardened clay as their primary building material. Clay was plentiful and they had a multitude of workers (slaves) to make the bricks and build their buildings. The major drawback of clay bricks was that they were not very strong or long lasting.

The Egyptians also used clay bricks, but mixed straw with the clay to give it added strength. Later, they mixed gypsum with the clay to further increase its strength and long lasting properties. It was this mortar-like substance, which they used to coat the surface of their pyramids and may still be seen today. Later, the Greeks improved upon the Egyptian mixture, but still fell short of Roman standards. Up until this time, finely cut and fitted stones were used for the construction of large permanent structures.

The Romans were the first to manufacture true cement, equivalent to the cement in use today. They mixed crushed limestone with volcanic ash from the base of Mount Vesuvius. They burned it and crushed the residue into a fine powder or cement.

Since the city of Pozzuoli was nearby, it was called Pozzuoli cement. When mixed with water and made into a paste, it could be formed into almost any desired shape. Then, when allowed to set, it became as hard as stone, i.e. concrete. The Romans used it to build coliseums, palaces, roads, and aqueducts, some of which are still standing. Using this Pozzuoli cement, the Romans were considered to be the world's greatest engineers and builders for almost 2,000 years.

Then came a truly ironic twist in the history of cement. With the fall of the Roman Empire, the art of manufacturing and using cement vanished. It disappeared for almost 1,000 years and was unknown in the Middle Ages.

About the late 1700's a number of individuals in Europe experimented with different mixtures and materials in an effort to produce a building material, which would not be weakened by water. Some historians claim that John Smearton, in England, was the first to discover what is generally known today as Portland cement. He mixed crushed limestone with specific amounts of clay. It is recorded that in England in 1790, this type of mixture was used to build a lighthouse. The old lighthouse kept disintegrating because of the humid atmosphere and salt water intrusion.

However, it was not until 1824 that the first patent was issued for Portland cement. It was issued in England to Joseph Aspdin. Legend has it that he named it Portland cement because the finished product resembled the stone of his hometown on the island of Portland.

At this point, it is deemed appropriate to distinguish between Portland cement and natural cement. Basically, they are both the same. However, in natural cement the exact ingredients needed are found in nature already mixed. In Portland cement, the ingredients are found separately and must be mixed artificially to the exact proportions in order to produce cement.

The basic manufacturing process is quite simple. The ingredients, when super heated, become a cinder-like substance called "clinker." The clinker, when ground into a fine flour-like powder, becomes cement. The cement, when mixed with water and allowed to set, becomes rock hard and is called concrete. In earlier times, the term "hydraulic" cement was often used. Hydraulic simply means that water must be mixed with cement powder to produce concrete and can be applied to both Portland cement and natural cements.

If only water was mixed with pure cement, the end product would have maximum strength, but would be very expensive. To reduce costs and to expand its volume, cement is usually mixed with less expensive fillers, such as sand and gravel. The sand and gravel aggregate add nothing to the strength of the concrete. In fact, if too much is used, the concrete will become too weak for most uses. At the end of the 19th Century, steel and reinforcing bars were added to the concrete to give it additional strength. This, along with the concept of "prestressing", constitute another scientific field and because of their late appearance, are not germane to the issues involved in this book.

As mentioned earlier, around the 18th century, a Portland-type cement was being produced in Europe, but in limited quantities. If there was a need for cement in the United States, it had to be imported and was very expensive. All of this changed during the construction of the Erie Canal (1817-1825).

At that time, there were few engineers in the country who knew how to build a canal. Those who were available had gone to Europe, mostly England, for training or to simply observe how it was done. It was there that they learned of the usefulness of Portland cement or hydraulic cement as it was called at that time. Cement was absolutely essential for the construction of the Erie Canal. The canal was to be very long (365 miles), had many locks (83), and required enormous quantities of water.

Something had to be used to stop the perennial leaks in the levee and locks.

In 1818, Canvass White, one of the engineers who had gone to England to study, discovered a deposit of clay-bearing limestone which, when super heated and ground into powder, became cement. It was in Madison County, New York, along the route of the Erie Canal. He used the cement, mixed with aggregate, to prevent serious leakages along the route of the canal. In this manner, the canal was constructed of materials, which were locally available. This was the first instance of manufacturing cement in the United States in commercial quantities. Canvass White patented his process, calling it hydraulic cement.

One of the problems associated with this initial discovery was its location. It was fine for the construction of the Erie Canal, but difficult for further commercial exploitation. The only source for fuel needed to super heat the limestone was the local forest. Initially, this did not cause much of a problem, as the entire area was covered with trees of all types. As more and more wood was being used as fuel and for construction purposes, the close-in supplies were being exhausted. Trees had to be cut and wood had to be hauled greater and greater distances. The few wagon tracks and trails in the area did not make the hauling of wood an easy task. Coal, which was a more desirable fuel, was not locally available.

About the same time, 1818, a blacksmith in High Falls/ Rosendale discovered that the limestone in his area also contained the proper amounts of clay and alumina . As explained earlier, he also discovered the ability to manufacture natural cement. However, because of its location, he too was unable to manufacture it in significant quantities, and marketing it presented insurmountable logistical problems. As a result, no effort was made to commercially exploit his discovery until later.

In order to gain a better knowledge of Rosendale cement, it is necessary to review how it was mined, manufactured, and marketed. It was these factors which later gave Rosendale an advantage and made it great. Conversely, it was also these factors which later contributed to its demise.

First - Mining: Rosendale was blessed in that it sat on top of a 30+ square mile deposit of naturally perfect limestone or "gray gold." It was also fortunate that the deposit was near the surface. In some places, the surface dirt was simply swept away, and the limestone was mined, open pit or quarry style. In other areas, there were out-croppings of limestone, where the veins sloped gently underground at a slight angle of only about 5 to 10 degrees. In this instance, the miners followed the vein from the surface to as far underground as they desired. There was no need for deep vertical shafts with numerous lateral tunnels. Other miners simply bored tunnels into the sides of mountains to obtain their limestone. As a result, almost everyone in Rosendale, who had a few acres of land, had their own mining operation. Survey maps indicate that there were over 200 such mines, pits, and quarries in Rosendale.

Next – Manufacturing: Manufacturing was a relatively simple two-step operation: burning and grinding. During the 19th Century, burning was done in vertical kilns. After a few rudimentary experiments, a fairly standard design was adopted. It was built of stone in the form of a large cylinder standing on end. Usually, it was encased within a mound of embanked soil to permit loading from the top. It was fire-brick lined, 10-15 feet in diameter, and about 20 to 40 feet in height. There was an entrance at the bottom, usually arched, which could accommodate men with shovels, forks, and rakes.

For burning, the kiln was filled from the top, first with a layer of wood/coal, then with a layer of limestone, then a layer of wood/coal, etc., all the way to the top. It was ignited from the bottom and let burn for 5 to 10 days. The draft from the entrance at the bottom, upward through the layers of limestone, wood/coal, acted as a bellows in a blacksmith's forge. It caused the wood/coal to super heat the limestone to about 1500 to 1800 degrees. The super heating converted the limestone into clinkers. When the cooking was completed, the residue was removed from the entrance at the bottom. The cinders were discarded; the clinkers were sent to a mill for grinding.

Most mining operators had their own kilns (close to their mines). However, many of the smaller mine operators hauled their clinker to one of the large consolidated grinding mills. The proliferation of kilns was so great that the remains of at least a hundred of them can still be found in the Rosendale area.

(Photograph from J. Maylie Collection)

VERTICAL KILNS – CENTURY CEMENT COMPANY
Rosendale, NY

The term "wood/coal" was used to describe the fuel for the kilns. Initially, wood alone was used. Later, it was used only to ignite the coal. The available supply of wood was not unlimited, and further, coal was much more efficient. Coal was absolutely essential if cement was to be manufactured in the large commercial quantities needed to meet the growing demand. It was the lack of an adequate supply of cheap coal that limited not only Rosendale, but also Canvass White's production of cement. The most feasible solution to the problem was to dig a canal from New York to the coalfields of Pennsylvania. This need was met when the Delaware and Hudson (D&H) Canal was completed.

The D&H Canal gave an overwhelming advantage to Rosendale. Using the D&H Canal, Rosendale was closer to its source of supply than its competitors; therefore, its coal was less expensive. Also, during periods of shortages, such as after a particularly hard winter, Rosendale would have priority in its use. Priority was assured because entrepreneurs from the area were also investors in the canal, as well as the coal fields of Pennsylvania.

The second step in the manufacturing process was grinding the clinker into cement. For cement to be effective, it had to be ground into a fine powder, similar to flour. One test required that it pass through a sieve which could hold water. Actually, the early grinding of clinker was done in water-powered grist mills, during periods when they were not busy grinding grain. It was in the grinding process that once again Rosendale took a giant leap forward.

In 1828, coincidental with the opening of the D&H Canal, a very large grinding mill was built, specifically designed for the grinding of clinkers into cement. It was located at the confluence of the Walkill River and the Rondout Creek. Its capacity and output was so large that soon all natural cement was being referred to as Rosendale Cement, a term that continued well into the 20th Century.

The final factor was marketing. This involved creating a demand, packaging, storage, sales, and distribution. Again, Rosendale cement was fortunate in these regards.

By its very nature, cement created its own demand. The producers of Rosendale cement merely had to let potential users know that their cement was available, that Rosendale cement was less expensive, and that they could deliver it more rapidly than other producers. This was accomplished with little trouble through the media outlets of the day.

Packaging was not as simple a task as it may seem. Since cement had to be kept totally free from moisture, it was shipped in barrels. The standard barrel contained 376 pounds of cement. Today's standard retail container is a bag (94 lbs., 1/4 of a barrel). The barrel was shaped similar to an old wine barrel, which bulged in the middle. The beauty of its shape was that one barrel of cement, despite having a gross weight of over 400 pounds, could be easily handled (tipped, rolled, steered and upended) by one person. Manufacturing barrels gave rise to an extensive local cooperage industry. Again, Rosendale was fortunate. The wood needed for the barrels came from the almost endless forests along the Delaware River on the New York and Pennsylvania border. Wood/lumber was the second largest commodity shipped on the D&H Canal.

The final steps of marketing were sales and distribution. As with the other factors, Rosendale, here too, enjoyed an advantage, especially in shipping. In the early 19th Century, the only alternative to the canal boat was the horse and wagon. The horse-drawn wagon could safely haul only about 1-5 barrels of cement, while the canal boat could carry 75-100 and later 200. Further, canal boats from Rosendale had water connections to the Mid-West, via the Erie Canal, and to ships sailing to all ports on the Atlantic coast and around the world.

Courtesy: Century House Historical Society, Rosendale, NY, Dietrich Werner, Pres.

Cooperage (cement barrel factory)

Throughout the 19th Century, Rosendale cement was the most widely used cement in the United States. It was used to build the Brooklyn Bridge, the Croton Reservoir system, the foundations of the U.S. Treasury Building, the Capitol of the United States, the U.S. Patent Office, and the Statue of Liberty. By mid-century, it was estimated that about 60% of all cement produced in the United States was produced in Rosendale. By the end of the 19th Century, Rosendale was producing over 4,000,000 barrels of cement a year. All of this came slowly to a halt during the 20th Century. However, before ending, it had played its role in making possible the tremendous industrial revolution of New York during the 19th Century.

The chief culprit in the demise of Rosendale cement in the 20th Century was the "rotary kiln." It was first introduced in England around 1886. Its acceptance in the United States was slow, but once accepted, it swept away all competition. Even Thomas Edison was granted a patent for a rotary kiln.

The rotary kiln was a long horizontal cylinder about 10 feet in diameter. It was 100 to 500 feet in length and was lined with fire brick walls and interior baffles. The cylinder was inclined slightly and rotated about three –quarters of a turn per minute. A hot flame was forced through the cylinder. The limestone was fed into the high end of the cylinder and super heated by the flame. The resultant clinkers emerged from the low end of the kiln, ready for grinding. There was no need to separate the cinders from the clinker. The rotary kiln could be operated on a continuous basis, and it took less than a day for the limestone, which was fed into one end, to come out as clinkers from the other end.

Besides efficiency in operations, the process permitted the insertion of exact amounts of additives, which could give Portland cement properties not possible with Rosendale cement. There was no relying on Mother Nature to provide the proper ingredients, and almost any low grade cheap limestone could be used. However, the greatest advantage of Portland cement was that its concrete could set (harden) in a matter of hours; whereas, concrete made from Rosendale cement required days before the forms could be safely removed. Although concrete made from Rosendale cement had greater tensile strength, it could not meet the demands of today's requirement for ever increasing productivity.

Of course, Rosendale cement could be manufactured using a rotary kiln. But why? It was no longer cost effective and its demand, even for special purpose usages, was negligible.

Courtesy: Century House Historical Society, Dietrich Werner, Pres.

Lawrenceville Cement Co.'s Works,

Rosendale. C1875

Detail from an Engraving based on a photograph by D.J. Auchmoody

To summarize, Rosendale cement dominated the cement industry in the United States during the 19th Century. It did so because Rosendale was located on a 30+ square mile deposit of the gray gold necessary for its manufacture. Also, it had direct access to a large transportation infrastructure essential for its manufacture, marketing, and distribution. Because of the Delaware & Hudson Canal, it had a reliable source of cheap coal. Without this massive supply of coal from Pennsylvania, not only Rosendale cement, but the industrialization of the state of New York would have been severely curtailed. Coal and its role in the industrial revolution will be discussed in the following chapters.

CHAPTER V

COAL

It is an accepted economic fact that in the 19th Century, coal was the fuel that was used to power the world's industrial revolution. Without coal, there would have been no industrial revolution worthy of note.

The energy derived from coal originated in the sun. For millions of years, the sun shined upon the earth, and its energy was absorbed by the trees and plants through a process called photosynthesis. Over time, the earth's vegetation withered, fell to the ground, and decayed. As it rested on the ground, it was covered with dirt, stones, ice, and water which compressed the decayed matter. When glaciers and floods receded, the entire process was repeated. Eventually, the compressed matter became coal, and with each new cycle, another seam of coal was formed. The heavier the weight of the covering material and the longer the matter was compressed, the more dense the coal became.

Depending on the definition used, there are four basic types of coal:

PEAT, such as found in the bogs of Ireland is the youngest and softest of coals. It has the consistency of moist clay and is used primarily for home heating.

LIGNITE, is the next in age and has the thickness and hardness of shale, or soft stone. There are billions of tons of lignite coal in the world. It is estimated there is a two hundred year supply in western United States alone. From it are extracted fuel oil, tars, and other useful chemicals. Some estimate that if the price of imported oil rises above sixty dollars a barrel, the extraction of fuel oil from lignite will increase rapidly since the end product could then be marketed at a competitive price.

BITUMINOUS coal (popularly known as soft coal) is the next oldest and most plentiful in the world. The United States, Russia, China, Canada, and Australia have most of the world's resources, about 400 years' supply. Today in the United States, most of it is used to generate electricity, to manufacture iron and steel, and for conversion into chemicals. One interesting note concerning the coal industry in the United States is that it is so fully automated that coal can be mined in West Virginia, shipped to Norfolk by rail, sent to Europe by ship, and sold at a price competitive with locally mined coal.

ANTHRACITE is the oldest and hardest of coals and is the primary concern of this book. In its formation, sometimes an added factor was introduced. It was the shifting of the earth's surface or mountain building. This additional compression was so great that the coal became "stone" hard. This severe squeezing created another advantage. It squeezed out most of the impurities, leaving a coal of almost pure carbon and oxygen. With little or no extraneous matter, it became a very clean burning coal.

From the records of ancient Greece and Rome, it appears that they had discovered coal, but made only limited use of it. The first widespread use of coal was in China. By the year 1000, it was their leading fuel. This was understandable since China was not heavily forested; hence, firewood was not plentiful. The use of coal in China was one of the marvels that Marco Polo wrote about during his travels.

Around the 1600's, there began an increased use of coal in the western world. This coincided with the thinning of local forests.

From 1600 until 1800, England led the western world in the use of coal. Legend has it that one of its earliest uses was to heat and dry malt. Then they tried to make beer with the malt thus dried, but the flavor of coal remained in the malt and beer. Later, it was found that by pre-heating the coal in a sealed environment, they could eliminate the flavor of coal in their beer. By thus pre-heating the coal, they discovered "coke." They used this coke to make iron and steel; thus, the industrial revolution was born.

England also pioneered in the use of coal for home heating and to power their steam engines. Originally, they used wood for these purposes, but as the supply of wood dwindled, they turned more and more to coal, i.e., bituminous coal. As a result, coal became the preferred fuel for both home heating and industrial use. This happened despite the fact that bituminous coal was smoky, dirty, and contaminated the environment. This was an era when chimney sweeping was a flourishing occupation in England.

Initially, charcoal (derived from wood in much the same manner as coke was derived from coal) was used to make iron and steel, but as wood became more scarce, it was replaced with coke. In the early years, coke was made by building a mound of coal, covering it with clay, and then igniting it. When it finished cooking, the mound was destroyed and the coke removed. This procedure was time consuming and wasteful. In the early 1600's, a beehive oven was developed, which could be used repeatedly and was much more efficient. By the year 1800, all blast furnaces in England were using coke to make iron and steel. The use of coke and coal for industry and home heating was so prevalent in England, that by 1800, they were mining over 2,500,000 tons of coal annually. The rest of Europe was not far behind.

From the above, it can be derived that at the end of the Middle Ages in Europe, the following sequence of events took place:

There was a general reduction in the supply of wood.

Greater use of coal as a substitute took place.

The introduction of the beehive oven further increased the use of coal.

The availability of coke accelerated the manufacturing of iron and steel.

The scarcity of wood also increased the use of coal for home heating.

Energy derived from coal was replacing energy derived from humans, animals, windmills, and waterwheels.

All of the above, made coal the new source of energy for the western world.

In the United States, there were vast deposits of coal. Strangely, until the Revolutionary War, most of the coal used in the colonies was imported from England. The basic reason for this was that the coal deposits in the United States were in the Appalachian Mountains, and there was no suitable means of transporting it to the eastern seaboard, where most of the settlements were located. Further, there was not a great demand for coal at that time since there was an almost unlimited supply of wood close at hand. What need there was for industrial power, was provided by water wheels in New England and windmills in Pennsylvania.

In the journals of the early explorers, LaSalle and Marquette among others, it had been recorded that there was a very limited use of coal by the Indians. They obtained it from outcroppings and used it for cooking and for heating their tents and wigwams.

It was not until after the Revolutionary War that the colonist made attempts to mine the coal in significant quantities. As the supply of coal from England was interrupted during the Revolutionary War and the War of 1812, more serious attempts were made to mine coal.

It started in the Appalachian Mountains of Virginia, Maryland, and Pennsylvania. However, by the year 1793, only 63,000 tons of coal were mined in the entire United States. The big problem was transportation. The horse and wagon was not a cost effective way of moving coal, especially through the mountains.

Coal production increased gradually during the early years of our nation. Then three situations arose, which caused a rapid increase in the mining and use of this natural resource. The first was the building of a network of canals to transport the coal. The second was the introduction of the steam engine, initially for the powering of steamboats and later for powering factories. The third was the universal acceptance of anthracite coal in the United States for home heating.

About 99% of all US anthracite coal came from three fields in the Wilkes-Barre, Scranton, and Pottsville areas of Pennsylvania. Its presence was known by the early settlers because of the many outcroppings. It was called "stone" coal because it was hard as stone. Since it was difficult to ignite and once ignited, was difficult to keep burning, it was largely ignored. It took a roaring wood fire to ignite anthracite coal, and if one had a roaring wood fire, why switch to coal, especially if there was a plentiful supply of wood nearby. Also, anthracite coal came in all sizes from pebbles to watermelon size chunks. It did not disintegrate into smaller size chunks as easily as bituminous coal. Crushing it into uniform small combustible sizes came later with the advent of steam powered crushing machinery.

The first recorded use of anthracite coal for home heating took place in Philadelphia around 1769. Little attention was paid to it until the end of the century. In 1802, one entrepreneur tried to bring a supply of anthracite coal to Philadelphia by floating it down the Delaware River in large wooden boxes placed on standard logging rafts. Of the six logging rafts so loaded, four were destroyed in the rapids, and only two made it to Philadelphia. Success did not come. Many of the buyers felt cheated, and rumor had it that the entrepreneur quietly slipped out of town.

Twenty-three years later in New York City, the story was a little different. It was recorded that on January 7, 1825, a group of investors gathered in the Tontine Coffee House on Wall Street. They witnessed a public demonstration of the successful burning of anthracite coal on a grate in a fireplace. The advantages of using anthracite coal for home heating were clearly demonstrated. It burned similar to charcoal, with a very hot glow and tiny blue flame. Also, it produced twice the heat of wood. Most important, it was relatively smokeless, and it left no odor or presence of soot in the house. It would burn with an even heat and over a much longer period of time. Its residue was a fairly clean white ash. There was very little need for chimney sweepers when burning anthracite "stone" coal.

What accelerated its acceptance even more was that at about this time there was an invention popularly known as the "$4 grate." When placed in a fireplace, it would cradle the coals about six inches above the stone floor. This permitted the air to circulate under the coals and pass up through the coals as they burned. This had the same effect as a bellows in a blacksmith's forge. By regulating the amount of air passing through the coals, one could regulate the intensity of the heat and the length of time the coals burned. With advantages such as these, the demand for "stone" coal skyrocketed. All of this came at an opportune time because the supply of locally available wood was becoming less plentiful.

In 1828, the use of air bellows in blast furnaces permitted for the first time the use of anthracite coal in the iron and steel making process. This had a multiplier effect on the demand for anthracite coal. It may be interesting to note that at that time, two of the nation's leading foundries were in New York (Troy and West Point). By the mid 19th Century, the demand for anthracite coal was greater than that of all other coals combined.

This insatiable demand for "stone" coal exceeded by far the capability of the nation's internal transportation infrastructure to move it. Bulk shipments of coal were handled by ocean going sailing vessels. Even the "Tontine" coal of Wall street fame had to be sailed out into the ocean and around the State of New Jersey. Unless a solution to the transportation problem could be found, the economic growth and industrial development of the nation would be severely limited.

The obvious solution was the construction of a viable internal canal system. Such a system was in place in Europe and especially in England. The following chapters cover the development of the internal canal system in the United States, with special emphasis on the Delaware & Hudson (D&H) Canal, the secret to New York's 19th Century industrial revolution.

CHAPTER VI

CANALS

Since the dawn of civilization, man has had an urge to travel in order to hunt for food, to seek greener pastures, or simply, to see what's on the other side of the mountain. He moved by foot and his impedimenta was carried by means of the backpack. Oddly, this method is still popular today, especially for recreational purposes. The legendary mountain men of the old west used it extensively. Even in the 20th Century there was the famous "Barefoot Mailman" of south Florida. He strapped a chair to his back and carried passengers over the sands and through the swamps along his 20-30 mile mail route.

Next, came the domestication of beasts of burden and the invention of the wheel. In terms of transportation, these had a tremendous multiplier effect. They expanded the horizons of mankind both literally and figuratively. About the same time, man began using the waterways (rivers, lakes, seas) as modes of travel. This further increased his ability to move people and goods over much greater distances and in much shorter periods of time. One can easily understand why the centers of the earliest civilizations were located in the proximity of natural waterways: the Nile River in Egypt, the Tigris and Euphrates Rivers in Babylonia and the Yangtze River in China.

The next challenge for mankind was how to extend the advantages of waterborne transportation beyond the banks and shores of the rivers and seas. Their solution was the canal, a ditch dug by man and filled with water. Ancient Babylon had canals connecting the Tigris and Euphrates Rivers. As early as 2000 BC, the Egyptians used canals to by-pass the cataracts on the Upper Nile. Darius the Great of the Persian Empire was credited with building a canal between the Red Sea and the Nile River, 2500 years before the Suez Canal. Ancient China used canals to help bind together its inward looking empire. Construction of its Grand Canal began about 600 BC and when completed was over 1000 miles long. By the year 1000 AD, it was handling about 2,000,000 tons of cargo each year.

For the western world, the building of canals remained fairly dormant until the stirrings of the industrial revolution. There was some canal construction here and there, mostly to improve natural waterways, but nothing of great significance until 1681. It was then that the French, under King Louis XIV, built the famous Canal du Midi. It was 148 miles long and connected the Bay of Biscay with the Mediterranean Sea. Ships could go from the Atlantic Ocean to the Mediterranean Sea without having to go around Spain and through the Straits of Gibraltar.

The next major canal was constructed in England by the Duke of Bridgewater. It connected his coal mines in Worsley with the developing industrial center of Manchester. It was privately financed and built, and its success made the Duke of Bridgewater one of the wealthiest men in England.

In England during the late 18th Century, the industrial revolution was just beginning. One problem was that they had plenty of coal, but no cost-effective way of transporting it to their newly developing industrial centers. Without great amounts of cheap coal to power their factories, their industrial revolution would have come to a grinding halt.

As a result of the financial success of the Bridgewater Canal, canal building in England began in earnest. They were fortunate in having abundant rain to provide water and few severe mountain barriers to overcome. In 1791 alone, the British Parliament authorized the construction of 81 canals over the next four years. The net result was that England became crisscrossed with canals and led the world in canal engineering and construction.

For purposes of this book, further discussion of canals will be centered around those built in the 19th Century and those classified as "inland" canals as opposed to those classified as "navigational" canals, such as the Suez and Panama Canals. Until the coming of the railroads in the mid 19th Century, there were no feasible and cost effective means of moving large amounts of cargo over long distances, other than by water. Because of the industrial revolution, there was an explosion of canal building. Without canals, it is estimated that the industrial revolution would have been delayed by about 100 years.

There are several factors concerning the building of canals which should be highlighted. First and foremost, a canal requires massive amounts of water. Next, the source of the water must be at a higher elevation than the canal and must be available on a constant and uninterrupted basis. One of the reasons the Erie Canal was so successful was that its source of water, Lake Erie, was 565 feet higher in elevation than its terminus on the Hudson River. In other instances, lakes which were at a higher elevation and along the route of the canal, were dammed and used as a source of water. Often, canals were built parallel to rivers and streams. These were interconnected by means of gated sluiceways, which could be opened or closed as needed to provide water for the canals.

Another requirement for a canal was that its bed be as nearly level as possible, with only a very slight slope of about one or two inches per mile. A slope with a steeper gradient would cause a current to flow at an unacceptable rate. Although the current would create an advantage when going in one direction, it would create an unacceptable impediment when going in the opposite direction, especially when canal boats were drawn by horses or mules. When greater differences in elevation were encountered, they were overcome by means of locks.

During the early days of canal construction, most locks were only about 10-15 feet wide, 70-90 feet long, and 8-10 feet high.

The lock consisted of a giant sluiceway built into the canal with two barriers or gates, one at each end. To go to a lower level, a barge would approach the gate on the high side, while the gate on the low side was in the closed position. Then the lock attendant would open the gate on the high side, permitting the water with the barge to flow into the lock. When the lock was filled with the water and barge, the lock attendant would close the gate on the high side behind the barge, sealing the water and barge in the lock. The lock attendant would then open the lower gate, permitting the water and barge to flow into the lower canal. To go in the opposite direction, the procedure was simply reversed. Since the height of the lock was usually about 8-10 feet, it would take about ten to twelve locks to compensate for about 100 feet difference in elevation. Passage through a lock took about ten to fifteen minutes.

Since the land surface over which the canal was to be built was seldom level, several different techniques were used. The most common was the "cut and fill" procedure, widely used today in the building of our Interstate Highway System. The procedure entailed cutting a wide trench type gap through a hill and using the residue to fill in the dips at the lower elevations. If the dip or valley was too deep, as when a river flows along the bottom, then it was crossed over by means of an aqueduct. An aqueduct was a bridge with a water-proof floor and high water-proof sides. When filled with water, the canal boats simply floated across it to the canal on the other side. In marsh lands, such as encountered along the Mohawk River when building the Erie Canal, the dirt was scraped from the surrounding areas to form banks along the route of the canal. The bank on one side had to be wide enough to accommodate the horses or mules pulling the canal boats. Since the early canals were only about four feet deep, the banks did not have to be too high.

High mountains with large rock formations were a serious problem. If an adequate water supply at a higher elevation was available, the mountain was crossed by building a large number of closely spaced locks to ascend and descend it. For mountains with gentler escarpments, inclined planes were used instead, much as the Egyptians used to move the enormous stones with which they built the pyramids. To cross a mountain, a canal boat was pulled out of the water on to a cradle. The cradle containing the canal boat was then pulled along the inclined plane or roadway, up over the mountain, and let down gently on the other side. To facilitate such movement, some of the larger boats were built with detachable sections. Prior to being hauled out of the water, the sections were disjoined. Then the individual sections were portaged over the mountain and rejoined into a single boat when let back into a canal on the other side.

When necessary, a tunnel was bored through the mountain, which permitted a canal to flow through it. The Main Line Canal in Pennsylvania had three such tunnels.

During the early canal building era, the surveyors and engineers had a difficult time determining the exact elevations of points along the canal route. They were good at pinpointing locations and determining distances and directions on a map. However, arriving at exact elevations over long distances was a different matter. Without accurate elevations, it was difficult to determine canal gradients and almost impossible to estimate canal construction costs. The English solved the problem with the invention of the Wye level. Basically, it was a spirit level mounted on a telescope in a very precise manner. The first one brought to the United States was used to survey the route for the Middlesex Canal in Massachusetts. This instrument was of vital importance to canal construction in the United States, since many canals were over 100 miles long, as well as being in uncharted areas.

In the United States, the early canal boats were of the Durham class. Unlike today's barges, which are large rectangular affairs carrying a thousand tons or more, the Durham canal boats were long and narrow, with rounded stems and sterns. They were

60-80 feet long, 9-10 feet wide, and carried 15-30 tons. They had to be narrow in order to pass through the narrow locks and to pass one another when going in opposite directions. The 15-30 ton limit was about what one horse or mule could pull safely. Also, the original canals were only about 4 feet deep. Later, the canals were deepened and widened to accommodate barges carrying 100 tons or more and were pulled by teams of horses or mules.

The animals were stabled in the bow of the canal boat, normally two per boat. They pulled for six hours and rested for six hours. Crew quarters were in the stern. The crew (3 or 4) consisted of a driver to lead or ride the pulling horse, a helmsman to steer the boat, and a cook/housekeeper. If possible, a general handyman was added to clean the stable, feed the horses, and generally keep the boat, ship-shape. The fourth person also provided relief to the others. A family of four made an ideal crew for a canal boat.

Canal boats were limited to four miles per hour, and packet boats (passengers only) were limited to 6 miles per hour. Faster speeds would have created high wave action, which would have eroded the banks, causing leaks and breaks. This is why steamboats were not permitted on the early canals.

This chapter was limited to the general nature of canals, especially during the early years. The following chapters will cover in greater detail canals in the United States, with specific emphasis on the Delaware and Hudson (D&H) and Erie canals. Today, the subject of inland canals may seem mundane, but in the 19th Century they were the queens of the transportation infrastructure.

CHAPTER VII

CANALS – USA

At the time of the American Revolution, there were no canals in the colonies. All major cities were either on the seacoast or on rivers and bays, with easy access to the ocean. The Appalachian Mountains, which stretch from Georgia to Canada, presented a barrier to interior east-west travel.

During the early period of our nation's history, when the Articles of Confederation were in force, the former colonies considered themselves to be independent states. They were so busy organizing themselves and enjoying the benefits of their new found freedoms, that there was little effort to promote industrial development, which would require the building of canals.

It was not until after the adoption of the new constitution that there began genuine feelings of "nationhood." They began to feel that there was a need to bind the nation together. They had gained the Northwest Territories (Ohio, Indiana, Illinois, Michigan and Wisconsin), and there was an urgent need to gain effective control over them. Routes of communication to these territories for travel and trade had to be established. This need became more critical after the Louisiana Purchase (1803). This further extended our boundaries westward and later with the cry of "54-40 Or Fight" they were extended to the Pacific Ocean.

At the national level, the two most prominent driving forces were "republicanism" and "nationalism." To Jefferson, the term "republicanism" meant to give priority to the small, independent and self-sufficient farmers. To Hamilton, it meant to give priority to the landowners and merchants. However, they were both strong advocates of "nationalism." In order to bind the nation together with roads and canals, both men were hampered by their belief that this was a "state" responsibility.

They felt that a constitutional amendment was needed before the federal government could provide funds for these purposes. Federal funds for such purposes were vetoed by Presidents Monroe, Adams, and even Jackson. (How times have changed!) Presidents Washington and Jefferson had similar beliefs, despite the fact that they strongly promoted "nationhood."

In his correspondence, George Washington emphasized the theme that "canals were fundamental to nationhood." He himself was deeply involved in the Potomac (later Chesapeake & Ohio) Canal. It tried to open up a route to the West by going up the Potomac River, through the Cumberland Gap, and on to the Ohio River. George Washington reasoned that this was the shortest route from the West to the Atlantic Ocean, and it would have made Washington, D.C and Alexandria, Virginia thriving commercial centers.

In 1808, Albert Gallatin, Jefferson's Secretary of the Treasury, prepared the first national and all-encompassing plan for the improvement of canals and roads to help bind the nation together. However, it was the War of 1812 that forcibly demonstrated the need for canals as well as road improvements. Large quantities of goods had to be able to move on interior routes of communication, which would be free from interdiction by hostile naval powers. In 1819, John C. Calhoun, Secretary of War, enlarged upon the Gallatin plan and even proposed that canal construction be placed under the supervision of the Army Corps of Engineers.

About this time, canal construction in the United States began in earnest. There was a literal explosion of canal building activity during the period 1820 to 1860. The way was led by the state of New York, with the building of the Erie Canal (1817-1825).

The Erie Canal was such a large project and so successful that it became the envy of the other states, as well as a training school for almost all of the early canal engineers.

What facilitated the building of the Erie Canal was the fact that the Mohawk River created a gap through the Appalachian Mountains. It provided an almost water level route from Albany to Buffalo. Some of the early canal promoters claimed that since the gap was created by the Almighty, it was His will that they should build a canal through it.

So many books have been written about the Erie Canal, including its successor, the Erie Barge Canal, that further elaboration is not needed. Therefore, only a few of the vital factors will be included in this book, in order that the importance of the canal can be kept in perspective.

The Erie Canal was planned, designed, built, and funded by the state of New York. De Witt Clinton (10 times mayor of New York, 2 times governor, one time U.S. Senator, and presidential candidate) is generally considered to be the father of the canal. It was 385 miles long, had 83 locks, and went from Albany on the Hudson River, to Buffalo on Lake Erie.

The fact that the Mohawk River paralleled the canal helped considerably by providing an almost water level route for the canal. Also, being interconnected with sluiceways simplified the water supply problem. Earlier, a bypass had been built around the rapids at Little Falls making the Mohawk River navigable for almost 75 miles. This had the side effect of introducing a westward orientation to the early settlers and entrepreneurs.

It is interesting to note that the early proponents of the canal did not plan that it would extend all the way to Buffalo on Lake Erie. Initially, they wanted it to go only to Syracuse. This was important because of the enormous supply of natural salt at nearby Salina. They reasoned that they could tax the salt to help pay for the construction of the canal. It was estimated that during the early days of the canal, about 60% to 70% of all of the salt used in the United States came from Salina. As a historical footnote, this salt (from Old Fort

Schuyler/Stanwix of the Revolutionary and French & Indian Wars fame) was considered to be the source of wealth and power of the Iroquois Indians, the most dominant Indian nation in North America.

For a while, thought was given to turning the canal north at Syracuse to Lake Ontario, via the easily accessible Oswego River. Cargoes going westward could then be shipped across Lake Ontario to Niagara, portaged over the isthmus, and then shipped farther west over Lake Erie. Fortunately, wiser heads prevailed and construction of the Erie Canal continued all the way to Buffalo on Lake Erie.

All of this construction was not lost on the British in Canada. They began planning and building the Welland Canal. It was on the Canadian side of the Niagara River connecting Lake Ontario with Lake Erie. It by-passed Niagara Falls and eliminated the need for portage across the isthmus. Had it been completed a little earlier, it might have diverted midwest cargoes from New York City to Montreal.

The original canal, when opened in 1825, cost about $7,000,000, which was recouped within five years by means of the collection of tolls. Over its entire life, the Erie Canal earned a profit of over $40,000,000 (about 3.5 billion in today's dollars). This profit was over and above the enormous costs of subsequent improvements. These included deepening and widening the canal; enlarging the locks; building extensions and lateral canals to Pennsylvania, Lake Ontario, Lake Champlain, the Finger Lakes and beyond. When finished, there were over 850 miles of canals in the state of New York in the 19th Century. The Erie Canal was a veritable "cornucopia" of revenue for the state.

When it opened, there were about 2,000 canal boats, 9,000 horses, and over 8,000 canal employees working on the canal. In 1834, 18,000 boat arrivals were registered in Albany, and by 1837, the canal was handling over 1,000,000 tons of cargo annually. In 1850, 23,000,000 bushels of grain (1/4 of all produced in the nation) were carried on the canal. As early as 1836, over 36,000,000 feet of lumber were moved over the canal annually.

In addition to freight, passenger travel was also heavy on the Erie Canal. Until eclipsed by the railroads, just prior to the Civil War, about 100,000 people traveled the canal annually. It was not unusual for the Buffalo terminal to clear 1,000 passengers a day. Over a hundred packets (passenger barges) crowded the canals. The accommodations on some were a little primitive, while on others, they were quite plush. The early packets carried about thirty passengers, but the later ones carried over 100. The packets traveled about 4-6 miles per hour, slightly faster than the cargo barges and were given priority at the locks. Travel time from Albany to Buffalo was four to six days. Not only was thru-passenger travel popular, but there was also considerable "intra" travel as well. Canal travel was so popular that it was used extensively for outings, picnicking, and for plain leisure travel, in much the same way that Caribbean cruises are used today.

The story of the Erie Canal would not be complete without mentioning the celebration which took place when it opened. It was called "The Wedding of the Waters" and was the most spectacular event ever staged in the nation up until that time. It started with a flotilla of lavishly decorated barges traveling from Buffalo to Albany and then being towed by steamboats down the Hudson River to New York City. There, two kegs of water from Lake Erie were poured into the ocean, "The Wedding of the Waters." The flotilla then returned up the Hudson River, through the canal to Lake Erie, where a keg of ocean water was poured into the lake. The flotilla completed the round trip in ten days and on board was almost every dignitary in the nation. At every town and city along the way, there were speeches, bands, parades, and celebrations. The highlight of the event was the grand salute of cannons. The entire distance from Buffalo to New York City was lined with cannons, all within ear-shot of one another. When the flotilla began its journey, the first cannon roared its salute. The next cannon, upon hearing it, fired its salute, and so on all the way to New York, and then back to the starting point. The entire procedure, all the way from Buffalo to New York and back, took three hours and ten minutes.

The opening of the Erie Canal was the first major breakthrough in the opening of the West. The earlier introduction of Fulton's steamboat had a tremendous multiplier effect on the thru-put capacity of the Hudson River and Erie Canal transportation system. One could cite statistics indefinitely concerning the importance of this system on the "economic" development of our nation, but that will be left to the scholars and historians. This book will be limited to the role it played in the "industrial" development of New York. Specifics will be the subject of subsequent chapters.

Not to be outdone, Pennsylvania, which was seeking to retain its position as the premier state of the nation, embarked on a canal building frenzy. Initially, they started with short single purpose canals, such as the Schuylkill and Lehigh, to bring anthracite coal to Philadelphia and the Delaware River basin. When they saw the progress of the Erie Canal, they went all out in their efforts to complete their Mainline Canal from Philadelphia all the way to Pittsburgh. When completed, it was 395 miles long and had 174 locks, 49 aqueducts, 3 tunnels, and a 38-mile portage railway. At the portage railway, canal boats were disassembled, if necessary, and placed on cradles. Then they were hauled over the mountains and placed in canals on the other side to continue their journey.

In addition, Pennsylvania built numerous lateral and connecting canals, bringing their total mileage of canals to 934. They built canals to Ohio, New York, New Jersey, Delaware, and Maryland. Later, the first shipments of iron and copper ores from the West traveled these canals. As a result,

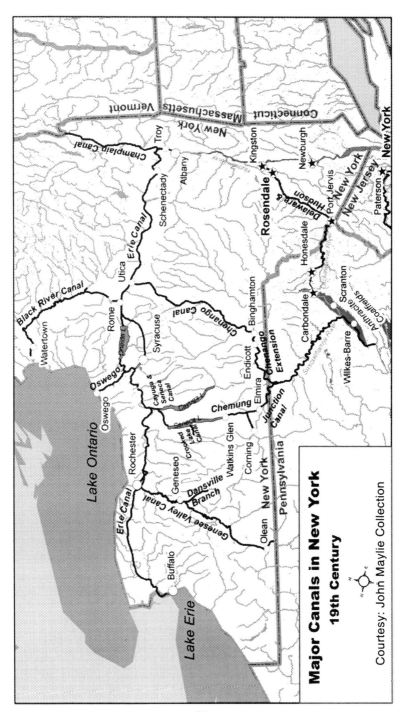

Major Canals in New York
19th Century

Courtesy: John Maylie Collection

Pittsburgh, with an abundance of coal locally, used these ores to become the iron and steel capital of the nation. By the end of the 19th Century, the Pennsylvania iron and steel complex was the largest in the world. This took place despite the fact that the canals in Pennsylvania were a financial disaster. Their canals virtually bankrupted the state and left them $57,000,000 in debt.

Both Virginia and Maryland tried to pierce the Allegheny Mountains, but with little success. Even the smaller states were not immune from the canal building mania. Rhode Island, Maine, and Connecticut built small canals to tap interior resources. A canal across the state of Delaware connected the Chesapeake Bay with the Delaware River estuary. This canal, along with the Raritan Canal and the Norfolk/Albemarle Canal, permitted boats to travel from North Carolina all the way to New England via an inland water route.

The Midwest was not to be outdone. Ohio had two canals from Lake Erie to the Ohio River. They also had two connecting canals to Pennsylvania. Indiana also had a canal from Lake Erie to the Ohio River. Illinois had a canal connecting the Mississippi River to Lake Michigan. It originated in Chicago, long before the latter became the meat and grain center for the nation.

Another interesting feature of the canal building era was that almost all of the promoters were individuals of means – landowners, merchants, politicians, and a few land speculators. At that time, it was not considered improper for an individual to purchase hundreds of thousands of acres of open land, sometimes for less than a dollar an acre, and vigorously promote the building of a canal, which might increase the value of his holdings. This was a period before "conflict of interest" laws were enacted, and people were expected to be rewarded for their efforts and foresight.

"Log rolling" or "pork barreling," as it is called today, was quite prevalent. Politicians were not above advocating canal building to out of the way places for the sole reason of gaining political support from the local inhabitants and to show that they "cared." Since many of these canals were not economically viable, they too turned into financial disasters.

Although the federal government did not give funds to the canal builders for their projects, it helped in other ways. The government made surveys for canal projects, calculated costs estimates for the canals, and made land grants to the builders. The latter was a program whereby the government would give the builders alternate sections of land, usually one mile square, along the right of way of the canal. The builders could then sell these sections to help pay for the cost of construction. It was a program which gained fame later, during the building of the transcontinental railroads.

In all, there were over 4,000 miles of canals built in the United States prior to the Civil War. Without the canals, the nation would have remained a loosely knit federation of sovereign states, squabbling among themselves, and seeking their own fortune. This almost led to open hostilities on a number of occasions. Not only did the canals help bind the nation together, but they were the only feasible means of transporting large quantities of goods at reasonable costs. This made possible the Industrial Revolution of the 19th Century. It was the Civil War which completed the process of industrialization, and of binding the nation together.

Now that the stage is set, we can proceed with the main purpose of the book: Rosendale, the Delaware & Hudson Canal, and the Industrial Revolution in New York in the 19th Century, making it the Empire State of the nation.

CHAPTER VIII

DELAWARE & HUDSON CANAL

PHASE I

This chapter could begin in a manner similar to the fairy tales of yesteryear. Once upon a time, there were four Wurts brothers: Maurice, John, William, and Charles. Two of the brothers, Maurice and William, were dry goods merchants in Philadelphia. At that time, Pennsylvania was the center of the Quakers in the United States. The Quakers were renown for their quiet, hard working, and no-nonsense way of life. Productive work was a "good" in itself, and they had an aversion to idleness. The Wurts brothers, although maybe not Quakers themselves, exemplified these characteristics and as a result, became the father and mother, heart and soul of the Delaware & Hudson Canal. Wurtsboro, New York, was named in their honor.

At this point, it should be mentioned that many excellent studies and books have been written about the Delaware & Hudson Canal, hereafter referred to simply as the D&H Canal. These contain a great amount of detail and minutia, and it is not our purpose to try and duplicate these outstanding efforts. It is intended that this book provide an overview of the D&H Canal, with just enough detail to confirm its role in making possible New York's industrial revolution.

During the period 1810-1820, Maurice and his brother William did much exploring (called back-packing today) in northeast Pennsylvania, especially in the Pocono Mountain area. They and their guide, David Noble, would be gone for weeks at a time, studying the countryside, catching fish for their meals, and generally communing with nature. During these trips, they encountered numerous out-croppings of black rocks, i.e., stone (anthracite) coal. The stone coal was ignored by almost everyone because it was difficult to ignite and burn. Also, why should they bother when there was an unlimited supply of wood nearby?

At first, Maurice and William were just curious to determine the limits of these out-croppings. One story has it that they had been given several thousand acres of land by the government in payment for supplies that they had given to the Continental Army. However, being of the merchant class, they were always on the alert for new business opportunities. They purchased many additional acres of land, some for as little as fifty cents an acre. Northeastern Pennsylvania was still a frontier and wilderness area with very few inhabitants.

Prior to their purchases, there had been only a few reported instances of anthracite coal being used in Philadelphia for home heating. As noted in Chapter V, roughly 99% of all anthracite coal in the United States is located in eastern Pennsylvania. It lies in three distinct deposits: the Schuylkill deposit in the southeast, the Lehigh deposit in the east central, and the Lackawanna deposit in the northeast. It was in the area of the Lackawanna deposit that the Wurts brothers did their hiking and made their purchases. About this time, some small quantities of anthracite coal from the Schuylkill and Lehigh deposits were finding their way into the Philadelphia market, but none from the Lackawanna deposit.

There were no trails or wagon routes to the northeastern deposits. The most common route of travel was by way of the turbulent Delaware River, which formed the border between Pennsylvania and its sister states of New York and New Jersey. Logging was the only occupation worthy of note in that area. The lumberjacks would cut timber during the fall and winter, and the logs would be assembled along the banks of the Delaware River. With the ice and snow of winter, it was possible to snake these logs to the river from significant distances. In the spring, they would bind or lash these logs into giant rafts. These rafts would then be floated down the

Delaware River to Philadelphia during the high waters caused by the rains and the spring thaws.

The above is mentioned because one spring, Maurice tried to send some of his stone coal to Philadelphia on one of these log rafts. The effort was unsuccessful because the raft struck a boulder, overturned, and the coal disappeared to the bottom of the river. They made another attempt to send coal to Philadelphia. They made a raft of pine boards and put their coal on it. Their idea was that once the coal reached Philadelphia, they would not only sell the coal but also the pine boards that made up the raft. In the spring, they tried to float their raft down Jones Creek and Lackawaxen River to the Delaware River, They did not get that far because their raft hit a boulder in Jones Creek and overturned, once more sending the coal to the bottom.

Around 1820, anthracite coal was gaining limited acceptance in Philadelphia for home heating purposes. About 325 tons had been shipped there from the Schuylkill and Lehigh deposits. The Wurts brothers were disappointed, as they saw their opportunity to supply the Philadelphia market vanish. Even if they got the coal there, they would not be able to compete successfully with the coal from the two closer deposits. Their only hope of recouping their investment was to try and capture the New York market. The city had not yet accepted the utility of anthracite coal. The brothers believed that they had the answer but their main problem was how to get the coal from their deposits to the markets in New York.

During this period, the entire nation was following the progress of that mammoth construction project in New York, the Erie Canal. The state of New York was building a canal from Albany on the Hudson River to Buffalo on Lake Erie. After considerable thought, the Wurts brothers concluded that the solution to their problem was to build a similar canal from their coal deposits in Pennsylvania to the Hudson River in New York.

Once again, the Wurts brothers went on extensive camping trips to reconnoiter possible routes for their canal. In Pennsylvania, the logical choice was along the Lackawaxen and Delaware River valleys to the Port Jervis area, at the juncture of New York, New Jersey, and Pennsylvania. However, from that point on, there were three possible choices. One route would go southeast, generally along the New York – New Jersey border, to the Hudson River near the Tappan Zee Bridge, about 20 miles from the city. The second route would go northeast, through the Shawangunk Mountains, across the Walkill River Valley to Newburgh on the Hudson, about 45 miles from New York City. Interstate 84 uses this route today. The third route would go north to Rondout/Kingston on the Hudson, about 95 miles from New York City. The term Rondout/Kingston is used because at that time they were two separate cities.

How could such a difficult and expensive canal be built? It was far beyond their means and that of their friends and associates as well. Further, it would require legal authorization from three different states, not always on amicable terms. It was at this point that the Wurts brothers pooled their resources, consolidated their efforts, and overcame seemingly insurmountable obstacles.

Learning from the now successful Middlesex Canal in Massachusetts, they gathered three groups of the most talented and capable people available to carry out their dreams.

One group was placed in charge of their Pennsylvania operations. It was headed by John Wurts. Being a state legislator in 1823, he quietly obtained a state charter authorizing his group to build whatever was necessary (canals, gravity railroads, bridges/aqueducts, slack water navigation systems, etc.), to ship their coal to New York. This authorization slipped through the legislature easily for three basic reasons: (1) at this time, Pennsylvania was in a canal building frenzy in an effort to compete with the Erie Canal;

(2) no state funds would be required; (3) the Schuylkill and Lehigh interests raised no objections, since it would ensure that the Lackawanna coal would not compete with their coal in the Philadelphia market.

The second group was formed in New York. It was headed by Philip Hone, a prominent politician who was Mayor of New York City and a prominent financier in the business circles of the city. In 1823, they obtained a state charter to not only construct a canal, but also to establish their own bank. Besides the political clout of the individuals involved, there were two other reasons why the New York state legislature was so agreeable. First, no state funds would be required. Second, although the Erie Canal benefited most of New York, those in southern New York felt "left out." The politicians seized upon this new canal as a cost-free way of showing that they "cared" for the citizens in the southern part of the state.

Once they were assured of New York state approval, the Wurts brothers set out to form their third group. This was the group that was to survey all feasible routes, prepare cost estimates, and design the system to be employed. Benjamin Wright was the Chief Surveyor and John Jervis was the Chief Engineer. Both were of Erie Canal fame and considered to be the best in the nation. The city of Port Jervis was named in honor of John Jervis. Benjamin Wright had the foresight to include on his team the services of an experienced geologist. After all, as far back as the Dutch colonial days, there were rumors of precious metals in the area. As a result of the findings of the geologist, the report recommended that, "water-lime stone ...equal to that used for constructing the Erie locks," be used to build the locks on the D&H Canal.

The first task of the survey crew was to recommend the best route for the canal. In Pennsylvania, there was not much debate. However, the route from Port Jervis to the Hudson River was a different matter, and it was at this point that Rosendale entered into the picture. As mentioned earlier, there were three possible options.

Option A was the shortest route, southeasterly to the Tappan Zee area. It was deemed feasible, but the deciding factor was that it would require approval of the New Jersey legislature. At this time, the relationships between New Jersey and its border states were strained. New Jersey was especially angry with New York because of the latter's claim of all of the Hudson River, right up the Jersey shoreline. In addition, the politicians of New Jersey decided that if a canal was to be built anywhere in the state, they would build it. Later, they did build two canals across the state, with mixed results.

Option B was a route generally northeast across the Shawangunk Mountains to Newburgh on the Hudson, similar to today's Interstate 84. It appeared to be the logical choice, since the Newburgh-West Point-Poughkeepsie triangle was a growing commercial center. It was almost as short as Option A and only about 45 miles from New York City. In addition, it was strenuously advocated by the two Orange County (Newburgh) representatives on the board. The only problem was going across the Shawangunk Mountains. It was determined that the most practical solution would be to build a tunnel through the mountains. The Pennsylvania Mainline Canal had three such tunnels. Some estimated that it would take five years to build the tunnels, but that was not a serious problem, since the charter allowed seven years.

It was fortunate that Option B was not chosen because no one could foresee the phenomenal growth of canal traffic, requiring a thru-put capacity of millions of tons of coal annually. The tunnel would have created an insurmountable bottleneck, which could have caused the financial collapse of the company. This happened in Pennsylvania, where even the deep pockets of state government could not save their Mainline Canal. Unknown to the members of the board at that time, the selection of Option B would have severely limited the industrial development of the state of New York, as will be explained later.

Option C was a route northward from Port Jervis, west of the Shawangunk Mountains and along the Rondout Creek Valley to Kingston on the Hudson, about 95 miles from New York City. At first, this did not seem to be a logical choice, since the Rondout/Kingston area was of little commercial significance. Also, why should their coal have to travel 215 miles to get to New York City when it was only 95 miles distant by direct measurement? Further, the canal would require over 106 locks, more than the entire Erie Canal, which was three times longer.

As mentioned before, an experienced geologist was a member of the survey crew. What he found was not "yellow gold," but "gray gold" along the Rondout Creek in Rosendale. The "gray gold" was a natural deposit of clay bearing limestone, containing the exact amount of ingredients so that it could be turned directly into cement. No exotic, expensive, and time consuming mixing procedures, such as used in Europe, would be required to manufacture cement.

Canvass White found a similar deposit along the route of the Erie Canal and used it to build all of their locks. In Chapter III, it was noted that the existence of "gray gold" was observed in Rosendale/High Falls in 1818, but no one was aware of how large the deposit really was. It was the geologist who made that discovery. The deposit was about 3 miles wide and 11 miles long. This deposit of 30+ square miles stretched from Rosendale/High Falls all the way to Rondout/Kingston.

Once the full extent of the deposit became known, it was a "no contest" situation. The two Ulster County (Rosendale) board members vigorously promoted the adoption of Option C. There was some indication that in Ulster County a loosely knit group was formed, which included some of the board members. It was reported that the group tried to secure mineral property rights for as much of the area as possible. It was noted that the Orange County (Newburgh) delegation muted their opposition to Option C. Whether they also became part of the group in Ulster County was not recorded. Again, it should be called to mind that this was long before our stringent conflict-of-interest laws were enacted and "private gain for the public good" was an acceptable norm.

A cement company was quickly formed in High Falls, and it was given a contract to supply all of the cement needed for the construction of the D&H Canal. By using this natural cement, construction costs were reduced, canal maintenance costs were kept to a minimum, and the canal experienced fewer operational interruptions.

As can be seen from the above and further clarified in the following chapters, without the discovery of the 30+ square mile deposit of "gray gold" in Rosendale, the D&H Canal might never have been built. Option A was not politically feasible. Option B was feasible, but would have turned into a costly failure. Option C, because of the enormous deposits of "gray gold," made possible one of the greatest success stories of the 19th Century.

The Wurts brothers now had the necessary charters from New York and Pennsylvania, and they had all of the board members in place. Their next task was to raise sufficient funds since neither state granted any funds for the canal. At this point, the business acumen of the Wurts brothers was displayed once more.

The brothers had arranged for a shipment of stone (anthracite) coal to be sent from Philadelphia via sloop around Cape May to the city of New York. On January 7th, 1825, they also arranged for a demonstration of their clean burning stone coal at the Tontine Coffee House located on Wall Street. They had invited all of the businessmen of the city to the demonstration. It was so successful that by 2 P.M., their initial stock offering had been fully subscribed.

Although the demonstration provided the much needed "seed money," they were still far short of their goal of almost two million dollars. They continued selling their stocks in the city, but they got an enormous boost from the banks in Ulster and Orage counties. This was the era before large national banks, and each of the local banks was able to tap directly into their European sources for additional funds.

By mid 1825, the Wurts brothers had all of the basic requirements in place and were ready to launch their project. One brother was responsible for all mining and canal activities in Pennsylvania. One brother coordinated financial and political activities in New York. One brother was deeply involved in canal construction and operations. The fourth brother could best be described as an "ambassador of good will." Although not directly involved, he handled odd requirements and generally promoted the canal in the appropriate circles.

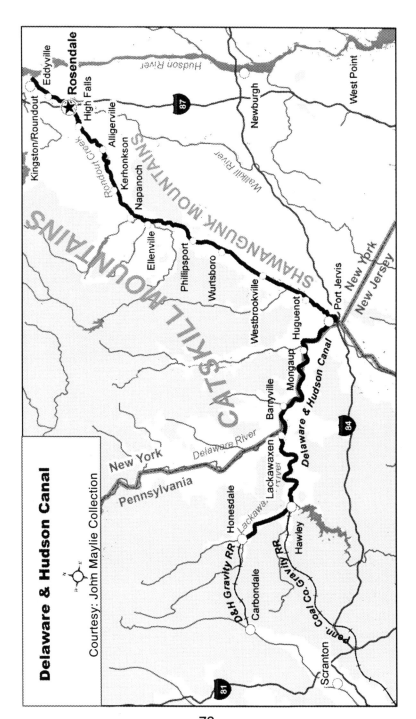

Delaware & Hudson Canal

Courtesy: John Maylie Collection

73

CHAPTER IX

THE DELAWARE & HUDSON CANAL

PHASE II

The Delaware & Hudson (D&H) Canal was 108 miles long and had 108 locks. It stretched from Rondout/Kingston on the Hudson River to Honesdale in Pennsylvania. From Honesdale, it was extended an additional 17 miles to Carbondale, by means of a gravity railroad. Originally, the canal was four feet deep, 20 feet wide at the bottom, and 32 feet wide on the surface. The locks were 8-12 feet high, 10 feet wide, and about 70 feet long. The early canal boats were of the long and narrow Durham type. Once the canal began operating at a profit, about 1833, they implemented a constant program of improvements. The canal was widened, the locks were enlarged, and the depth was increased to 6 feet. In the later years, it could accommodate barges of up to 130 tons.

From an engineering and/or historical viewpoint, there were two unique features which were invariably associated with the D&H Canal. One was the gravity railroad and the other was the Stourbridge Lion. Both of these were the product of the brilliant chief engineer John Jervis. He later won fame for many other projects, including the Croton Dam and water system for New York City.

The gravity railroad was used to close the seventeen mile gap between the canal terminal in Honesdale and the company coalfields in Carbondale. Between the two were the Moosic Mountains, rising almost 1,000 feet above the cities. John Jervis designed a system of inclined planes to go over the mountains. It consisted of a corduroy road on which were fastened two sets of rails – one for ascending traffic and one for descending traffic. This was before the introduction of the steel "T" rails, which were used later. In effect, they were really planks of wood, stood on edge, and upon which were fastened a steel ribbon. The coal carts rode on these wood/steel rails and were connected with a steel cable (produced by John Roebling of Brooklyn Bridge fame) in such a manner that the gravity force of the descending cart helped to pull up the ascending cart.

The Stourbridge Lion was a steam powered locomotive purchased in England and brought to Honesdale. John Jervis hoped to use it to pull the coal carts on the gravity railroad. Horatio Allen, his chief assistant engineer, drove it on the initial test run. Unfortunately, the wood/steel rails could not support the weight of the Stourbridge Lion. John Jervis then disassembled the Lion and used the stationary steam engine to replace some of the horses that were pulling the coal carts. Some historians claim that the test run of the Stourbridge Lion was the first time that a steam powered locomotive ever ran in the United States.

In 1823, the Pennsylvania and New York canal companies were united into the Delaware & Hudson Canal Company with Philip Hone as the president. In 1826, he resigned and John Bolton became the president. Mr. Bolton was very capable, energetic, and closely supervised all phases of canal construction. Construction began in 1825. The canal was officially opened on December 3, 1828, when a flotilla of canal boats carrying 120 tons of coal traveled its entire length.

Despite his extraordinary abilities, John Bolton was considered to be both extravagant and ostentatious. He had the company build him a mansion in Rondout, where he could supervise the construction of the canal. When the company was in serious financial difficulty in 1831, he was replaced by John Wurts. One of his first cost cutting actions was to sell the mansion.

John Wurts handled overall canal administration from New

York City. His brother, William, handled the Pennsylvania operations, while Maurice handled terminal and sales operations from Rondout/Kingston.

At this point in the history of the canal, there were two unique accomplishments worthy of note. First, its construction was completed within budget, and it was operational within three years, instead of the seven years allocated. Second, it was considered by many to have been the largest single, privately funded construction project ever attempted in the new nation.

As with any new large organization, there were significant growing pains. The most serious took place around 1830, after its first full year of operation. It seems that in order to get as much coal as possible into the new market, instructions were given not to waste time mining coal, but to ship all the surface coal that was immediately available. Philip Hone, still a board member, was blamed for this order. As a result, a lot of the coal shipped the first year – about 30,000 tons – was of inferior quality, containing debris, dirt, rocks, etc., mixed in with the coal. At that time, stone coal was still not widely accepted in New York. This initial shipment of inferior coal confirmed their suspicions and severely curtailed sales for the next few years. No doubt their competitors, the Schuylkill and Lehigh coal companies, who shipped their coal to New York via sloops and schooners, helped keep alive the stories of inferior Delaware and Hudson coal.

Despite the heroic efforts of the Wurts brothers, the D&H Canal Company became insolvent. It was rumored that one evening the board voted to actually cease operations. However, the next morning, Philip Hone pledged some of his personal funds to keep the canal operating.

It was at this time that once again Rosendale came to the rescue of the D&H Canal Company. The first instance was at the beginning when it played a pivotal role in the selection of the best route for the canal and in obtaining the necessary funds for its construction. At that time the D&H Canal Company was insolvent and even with the insertion of Philip Hone's personal funds, the canal could not continue to operate. The role that Rosendale played at this juncture was three-fold.

First, by 1830, the manufacture of Rosendale cement was going full blast. In Chapter IV, it was explained that in order to manufacture cement, the locally available clay-bearing limestone had to be super heated in giant vertical kilns. This process turned the limestone into clinker, which, when ground into a fine powder, became cement. Initially, wood was used for the super heating. When the canal opened, D&H coal was substituted for wood. Anthracite coal produced about 2 1/2 times the heat of an equivalent amount of wood. During this critical period, the Rosendale cement companies were the largest purchasers of D&H coal. This provided the canal company with much needed cash during a critical period.

Second, over one-half of all Rosendale cement was shipped to market via the D&H Canal and its terminal facilities. Although in its infancy, manufacture and sales of Rosendale cement increased at an exponential rate. This increase was so dramatic that by 1837 the White Cement Company alone was producing 600 barrels of cement each day. These cement shipments resulted in additional revenue for the D&H Canal Company.

Third, Rosendale cement gave birth to an enormous cooperage industry. This was before the advent of waterproof paper and plastic cement bags. Powdered cement has a very absorbent nature and can even absorb moisture from the air on damp days. Therefore, immediately after grinding, it was put into barrels and sealed. The cooperage industry required large quantities of properly seasoned wood. The wood came from the lumber industry along the Delaware River. So much wood was carried on the D&H Canal boats that one year, during this crucial period, the canal boats carried more wood than coal. Again, this provided the canal company with sorely needed revenue at a most opportune time.

Courtesy: Century House Historical Society, Rosendale, NY Dietrich Werner, Pres.

The New York Cement Company at LeFever Falls
Town of Rosendale Ulster County, NY

In the meantime, the Wurts brothers were doing their best to keep the company afloat, financially. Besides getting rid of the Bolton mansion, they sold the company's bank building on Wall Street. They retained only two offices on the second floor for their use. Parcels of land along the canal right-of-way were sold. They instituted a sales promotion campaign that would have made Madison Avenue proud. They guaranteed the quality of their product, offered to buy back the coal if the customer was not satisfied, and offered a "time payment" plan, if desired.

The Wurts brothers promoted the use of stone coal for purposes other than home heating, such as manufacturing nails, producing salt, smelting iron, and wherever the power of steam was needed. They expanded their sales market to include Boston, Hartford, and Providence in New England. One of their greatest successes was in convincing steamboat owners to use coal instead of wood. A typical sales pitch would promote the theme that 10 tons of coal ($100) was equivalent to 20 cords of wood ($240). They were so successful that by 1836, coal replaced wood as the primary fuel for Hudson River steamboats. An additional factor was that the coal did not have to be delivered to the boats. The boats simply stopped by the stockpiles of coal at Rondout/Kingston for their supply, while traveling up and down the river.

Courtesy: D.& H. Canal Historical Society, High Falls, NY

Mountains of coal at Honesdale
waiting shipment on
D&H Canal

With the Wurts brothers now in total control, solvency was regained, and in 1833, the company paid its first dividend. Outside negative factors (recession, cholera epidemic, etc.) intervened for a few years, but the company resumed paying dividends in 1837 and continued paying dividends for forty years. The dividends normally ranged from 8% to 18%. The banner year was 1845 when they paid a whopping 37% dividend and issued a 25% stock split. The D&H Canal Company quickly paid off the two minor loans, which were guaranteed by the state of New York, and in 1846, they closed their bank. The bank was no longer needed.

Another interesting feature of the D&H Canal Company was that it was our nation's first large "vertical" corporation. This was long before Standard Oil and U.S. Steel came into being. They owned the coal fields and mined their own coal. Also, they owned the means of transportation. They had their own storage and distribution system as well as their own sales and marketing organization. By mid-century, it was considered by some to be the largest corporation in the United States.

Around 1840, the Lehigh Coal Company, which was instrumental in keeping D&H coal out of the Philadelphia market, cast envious eyes on the New York market. They teamed up with New Jersey cross-state canal interests in an effort to flood the New York market with their coal. This time, the D&H Canal Company was aided, not by Rosendale, but by an unexpected benefactor. That summer, there were torrential rains and massive floodings in eastern Pennsylvania. These severely damaged the Lehigh mines and canals. It took them two years to repair the damage, and by then, the Lehigh Coal Company had lost interest in the New York market.

In the meantime, the D&H Canal Company continued its dominance of the New York City market. The fact that its Hudson River terminal was 95 miles north of the city also meant that it was only about 45 miles from Albany, a terminal for the Erie and (Lake) Champlain canals. This gave the

D&H Canal Company a "lock" on the entire central New York state market, the northern New York market, the Vermont market, and a strong position in the Canadian markets.

The phenomenal growth of the D&H Canal Company continued, and by mid-century, over one million tons of coal alone were being carried by the canal annually. Tonnage increased rapidly until the canal was handling over three million tons of coal each year. The company doubled the capacity of its gravity railroad by double tracking it, but even that was not sufficient to satisfy the demand for anthracite coal. Associates of the D&H Canal Company formed the Pennsylvania Coal Company, which opened coal mines south of Carbondale, near Scranton and Wilkes-Barre. From there, they built a separate railroad system to a D&H terminal at Hawley. It was so successful that they, too, had to double track their railroad, in order to meet the growing demands for anthracite coal in the New York markets.

In 1858, John Wurts, the last of the Wurts brothers active in the canal company, had to resign for health reasons. George Olyphant then became president. He kept things going steadily until 1869, when Thomas Dickson became president. It was then that the D&H Canal Company began to change. He realized that the days of the canal were coming to a close and that the future belonged to the railroads. He began de-emphasizing canal operations and began acquiring railroads. Where he could not find a railroad to buy, he built one. If he could not build a railroad, he formed partnerships, obtained leases, or made other business arrangements. The thrusts of his acquisitions were in northern Pennsylvania, all of New York state, and up into Canada. The railroads involved were too numerous to mention by name and are really not germane to this book since they merely continued the legacy left by the D&H canal, admittedly by a different means.

In the year 1898, only 500,000 tons of coal were carried on the D&H canal. Finally, in 1899, after carrying some small quantities of coal, the canal was abandoned. On June 13th of that year, the assets, along with its unpaid tax obligations, were sold to a Kingston combine. The coup-de-grace took place in 1899 when the company formally changed its name from the Delaware & Hudson Canal Company to simply the Delaware & Hudson Company.

As a service to one of its non-coal customers, the last 24 miles of canal from Napanoch to the Hudson River remained operational through 1900. In storybook fashion Rosendale would not let the canal die a quick death. The entire canal was purchased by Samuel Coykendall (Consolidated Rosendale Cement Company), and the final 13 miles from High Falls to Kingston/Rondout remained open another 13 years. It was used primarily to carry cement to market, and in some years, this short canal even made a profit.

(Photograph: From Coal Fields to the Hudson by Larry Lowenthal)

Lock #7, Delaware & Hudson Canal
Rosendale, NY

Footnote:
Author was born in the Lock Tender's House

It might be noted that the Delaware & Hudson Company flourished for many additional years, carrying coal on its railroads. It became one of the leading railroad companies in the nation. It had 895 miles of track in the United States and Canada. However, with the decline of the entire railroad industry after World War II, the fortunes of the D&H Company also declined. The Canadian portion went to the Canadian Pacific Railroad, and most of the U.S. sections were taken over by AMTRAK. The Delaware & Hudson Company finally closed its doors and ceased operations in 1987. In summary, Rosendale cement made possible the beginning of the Delaware & Hudson Canal Company. It was a key factor in saving the company from disaster during its formative years, and even in its demise, it prolonged the life of the canal for an additional 13 years.

The enormous quantities of coal carried by the D&H Canal provided the fuel to power New York's 19th Century industrial revolution. Without the coal, the industrial revolution would not have taken place, or at best, it would have been very limited. Pennsylvania would have assumed the dominant role in the industrial development of the nation. New York would have continued its development in a manner similar to the other coastal states, relying on the growth of its agricultural and trading business sectors. The reasons for this will be covered in the following chapters.

CHAPTER X

19TH CENTURY – ROSENDALE

Chapter III ended with the discovery of natural cement in the High Falls/Rosendale area by Nathaniel Bruce in 1818. Bruceville was named in his honor. However, it was not until April 26, 1844, that there was an official "township" called Rosendale. Originally, the name of Rosendale was applied to a small settlement of three or four houses near the home of Jacob Rusten, the first settler. Today, it would be located near the intersection of State Roads 32 and 213. One supposition has it that the name Rosendale was derived from the name of a city in Holland called Rosendahl.

Basically, the state of New York is divided into 62 counties, including New York City, each with its own governing body. The counties, in turn, are sub-divided into cities and townships, each also with its own governing body. Sometimes, there are smaller sub-units called villages, but for purposes of this book, the term Rosendale will refer to the township, unless otherwise noted.

Once the canal became fully operational and the cement industry began to grow by leaps and bounds, the Ulster County government was faced with a problem. Tensions grew between the farming community on one hand and the mining and canal communities on the other. Their needs and their beliefs in the role of government were quite different. The rowdy and boisterous lifestyles of the miners and canal boat crews were in sharp contrast to the staid and quiet lifestyles of the farming community.

To alleviate the situation, the state of New York, in collaboration with the Ulster County government, detached the cement producing areas from the townships of Hurley, Marbletown, and New Paltz. The three detached areas were combined into a new township named Rosendale. This new township included the village/communities of Rosendale, Binnewater, Bruceville, Lawrenceville, Cottekill, Whiteport, Hickory Bush, Maple Hill, Tillson, LeFever Falls, Creeklocks, Bloomington, and parts of High Falls.

It is interesting to note that when the township of Rosendale was created, the largest single group of town officials was involved in law enforcement: five constables and three justices of peace. This group was followed by revenue officers (3 property appraisers and one tax collector). The next group of town officials was the three road superintendents.

There was one lone (no staff) school superintendent to oversee six one-room school houses and one two-room school house. One teacher was hired per classroom and taught eight grades or four grades, as in the two-room school house. Since many of the miners were without families and the canal boaters used their families as crew members, the overall number of students was not as large as would have been expected. Some old records indicate that the attendance rate for grade school was only about 50% to 60%. High school was available only in Kingston or New Paltz, 4 to 8 miles distant.

Our tale of 19th Century Rosendale will begin about 1825 when the full extent of the 30+ square miles of "gray gold" was realized. Prior to this time, there were only about 40 families in the area that later was to become the Township of Rosendale. Agriculture was their main occupation, and they lived on widely dispersed farms in a self-sufficient manner that would have made Thomas Jefferson proud. The families were large, at least four to eight children. Since farms were highly labor intensive only during planting and harvesting, this meant that at other times there was a surplus of labor. It was this surplus that provided about 70% of the labor force needed to construct the original D&H Canal. This not only gave the farm family an opportunity to earn "hard money," but some farmers actually became sub-contractors for the canal company.

Initially, this worked fine for the canal company since farms extended along the route of the canal, all the way to Pennsylvania. However, the newly emerging cement industry had to tap into the stream of immigrants flowing up the Hudson River on their way west through the Erie Canal. Immigrants with mining experience were especially sought after. As the cement industry grew, the demand for additional workers also grew.

After the D&H Canal became successful, it embarked on a massive canal improvement program. This required so many additional workers that they, too, were forced to tap into the immigrant stream of laborers. Because of these two demands, the mix of workers in the Rosendale area was reversed. By about 1840, only about 30% of the workers were of local origin, and about 70% were from the stream of immigrants. Most of the immigrants came from Ireland and Central Europe. The latter group was a diverse group, but for reasons known only to the local inhabitants, they were uniformly referred to as "Austrians."

It was around 1825 that the Rosendale boom began. The first effect was a period of acute land speculation. Those with means tried to buy or obtain mining rights to all of the clay bearing limestone in the area. Within a short time, all of the area that was later to be called Rosendale was "spoken for."

The second effect was the explosive growth of the natural cement manufacturing industry. It all began when John Littlejohn of High Falls was given a contract to supply all of the cement needed for the construction of the D&H Canal. This was a major cost saving feature for the canal because otherwise, they would either have had to import Portland cement, or use the more expensive natural cement from the Erie Canal area.

In the meantime, the entrepreneurs of Rosendale did not wait until the completion of the canal to begin their activities. Immediately, they began mining and manufacturing natural cement.

Before the coal from Pennsylvania arrived in Rosendale, the cement companies used locally available cord wood to super heat the clay-bearing limestone into clinker. At the confluence of the Rondout Creek and the Walkill River, they built one of the largest waterpowered grinding mills in the nation. The cement companies began marketing their natural cement along the Hudson River, all the way to New York City. It wasn't long before they marketed their natural cement up and down the Atlantic coast and even to foreign countries. The location of the cement companies in southern New York gave them a price advantage over similar cement manufacturing operations along the Erie Canal. The results of their marketing activities were so dramatic that by the mid-nineteenth century, all natural cement became known as "Rosendale" cement. Even to this day, some reference materials still consider natural cement and Rosendale cement to be synonymous.

The estuary, located at the confluence described above, had an excellent "slack water" capability. It was quiet, reasonably wide and deep, with an almost negligible current. The long level banks along the shores made it ideal for the stock piling of mountains of coal, as well as barrels of cement. It became the major distribution center for anthracite coal and natural cement in the nation. The storage of coal reached unbelievable proportions. Canal barges would unload their coal onto the banks quickly and then return to Pennsylvania for another load.

Some of the coal barges would be towed by tugs down the Hudson River directly to their New York City customers. Others would be towed directly to customers along the Erie and Lake Champlain canals.

The quick trips of coal barges back and forth to Pennsylvania resulted in enormous stock piles of coal on the banks of the Rondout estuary. One mountain of coal stretched for about 500-600 feet in length, was 50-60 feet high, and about 200 feet wide at its base. A pile of 100,000 tons or more of coal was not uncommon. This permitted the 1,000+ ships, tugs, boats and barges to tie-up along side a coal pile, load up quickly, and be on their way, sometimes in less than an hour. Although the D&H Canal was closed for 3-4 months a year due to snow and ice, the Hudson River south of Kingston was seldom closed for more than one or two months a year. One of the positive side effects of these terminal operations was that the Rondout estuary developed into a major boat and barge building and repair center.

An overview of cement in general was covered in Chapter IV. This chapter will be limited to the highlights of the Rosendale cement industry. Records indicate that there were about 19 major cement companies in Rosendale. Some of the larger ones produced as much as 600 to 1,000 barrels of cement a day. In addition, there were many smaller independent producers. Topographic maps indicate that there are over 250 abandoned mines in the Rosendale area.

These smaller producers had the option of burning the limestone in their own kilns or taking it to one of the larger producers who had banks of as many as 15-20 kilns. That many chose to burn their own limestone is indicated by the fact that the remains of many single and double kilns scattered throughout the area, may still be seen today. By the end of the 19th Century, there were about 5,000 people employed in the Rosendale cement industry. Cement had now replaced stone as the most popular heavy construction material in the nation.

The people of Rosendale were an interesting lot. From a broad demographic viewpoint, it could be said that they were divided into two general groupings. There was the merchant/farming group and the immigrant/laboring group. The former consisted of the descendants of earlier settlers and some recent arrivals from the New England states. The latter group consisted of the more recent European arrivals (mostly Irish and Austrians), who worked on the canal and in the cement industry. The former group were the community leaders and tended to dominate politics. They were the farmers; they owned the stores, shops, hotels, and they provided most of the professional services, such as doctors and lawyers.

In looking at the names of owners of various businesses at that time, there appeared to be only a sprinkling of Irish or central European names. A lone McGee was listed as the owner of one hotel and bar. Many hotels and boarding houses had their own bars. One survey of Lawrenceville indicated that there was one bar for every eight buildings. When scanning the list of workers in the mines and on the canals, it was found that they were heavy with Irish and central European names.

In the 19th Century, the most common non-boarding house building was the church. Protestant churches were the most numerous, with at least one in almost every community. The most dominant denomination was the Dutch Reformed, with the Baptist, Episcopalian, and French Huguenot (Calvinist) following. The Catholic church will be discussed later. These churches were the center of social as well as religious activities. Often political activities were included under the church umbrella.

Generally, all got along reasonably well and without major disruptions. The most serious breach of tranquility took place during the revolt of the tenant farmers around 1841. It did not affect the Rosendale cement industry directly, but the surrounding farmers were deeply involved. In one instance, the revolt ended in bloodshed. Finally, the New York legislature passed a law forbidding the practice of extended tenant farming.

There was one event which had serious consequences for the merchant class. In 1895, a fire started in the village of Rosendale and raged for the better part of two days. It literally destroyed over one-half of the village. Most of the shops, half of the homes, and even a couple of churches were burned to the ground. Luckily, there were no fatalities. This was before the age of FEMA, all of the other disaster agencies, and the current hordes of trial lawyers.

The residents simply absorbed their losses and went on with their lives. Despite the fact that the fire took place during the height of the cement boom, the production of Rosendale cement continued unabated. Under the category of lessons learned, it was recorded that shortly after the fire, the village of Rosendale established its first Volunteer Active Hose Company.

The other side (Irish/Austrian) of Rosendale, was perhaps a little more interesting. The Irish were renown for their hard work, and when the occasion arose, their belligerency. The Austrians, who were known for their hardheadedness, were determined not to be outdone. Both enjoyed a rousing Saturday night. Since most were recruited from the flow of immigrants coming through New York City, they were usually without families. Their basic plan was to earn enough money to send for a bride from the "old country." This heavily male dominated population tended to become well lubricated on Saturday nights.

A unique feature of both groups was that they were well indoctrinated in the Catholic faith and attended church services on a regular basis. Saint Peter's Catholic Church was by far the largest and most heavily attended church in Rosendale. As history records, it was adjacent to and became an intimate part of the renowned "Miracle of Rosendale."

After hearing many tales concerning the Irish and Austrian workers of Rosendale, one must conclude that the relations between the two were not always amicable. Stories abound as to how, on a Saturday night and after a few droughts of spirits, some of the more rambunctious Irish would come upon a lonely Austrian. Unless the Austrian could run fast, which he usually refused to do because of his hardheadedness, he would find himself in the canal. The following Saturday night, a group of Austrians would seek out some lonely Irishman, who would then also find himself in the canal.

A common method of initiating hostilities was to snatch a miner's bowler and toss it into the canal. One short feisty Austrian escaped this harassment by simply placing his small pearl-handled .38 revolver under his bowler when he placed it on the bar. He was fortunate in one other respect. Years later when an attempt was made to fire the pistol, it was so poorly made that it blew apart.

Another interesting feature of these happenings was that on the following day, Sunday, both groups dressed in their best, with all of their bumps and bruises, would attend mass at Saint Peter's Church, sometimes sitting side by side. The pastor, usually a native from Ireland, was faced with the undaunting task of keeping the peace without showing favoritism. This, they did in an admirable fashion. They were so successful that they had Irish and Austrians working together, shoulder to shoulder, building the largest church in Rosendale, nearly twice the size of its nearest competitor. They did this with their own hands, on a voluntary basis, and in the most difficult of terrain. They built not only the church, but also the rectory, the school, the surrounding roads, and the retaining walls.

It was on December 17, 1899, that the "Miracle of Rosendale" took place. The Joppenberg mountain, the highest in Rosendale, rising almost 500 feet, contained some of the best deposits of "gray gold." As a result, it was mined and tunneled-under from all directions and by several different cement companies. No one company had overall control. The mountain resembled a giant Swiss cheese, penetrated on all sides and from virtually every direction. The mountain was so undermined that on that fateful day, the entire mountain gave a loud audible rumble and collapsed, completely closing all tunnels and crushing everything within.

The "miracle" was that there were no fatalities. The collapse took place around noon, and the entire work force was outside having lunch (as told to the author by an eye witness who was standing about 100 feet from the point from which the photographs of the Joppenberg Mountain were taken). To this day, one can appreciate the enormity of this by simply standing on State Road 213 and looking at this huge pile of rubble that

BEFORE

Black Smoke Cement Mine "Joppenberg Mt" Rosendale.

Double picture shown, is a Stereographic photo.
When viewed thru a Stereoscope viewer a 3D image was displayed

AFTER

Joppenberg Mountain, Rosendale, NY

was once called a mountain. Giant boulders and rocks still break loose and on occasion come rumbling down onto the highway, into the old canal and Rondout Creek.

It was rumored that on the following Sunday, the pastor gave a very pointed sermon to his mixed congregation. Using the collapse of the mountain as a starting point, he stressed the need to reform and to become less violent. Indications were that it must have been effective because it was a long time before any of the miners again found themselves in the canal.

Oddly, it was about this time that the rotary kiln was beginning to make its presence felt in the United States. Construction engineers began switching away from natural cement to portland cement. The production of Rosendale natural cement began to decline from a high of about 4,000,000 barrels in 1900, to only about 300,000 barrels in 1910. By the year 1920, the population of Rosendale had fallen from a high of about 7,000 to only 2,000.

It is always sad to see the decline of a town such as Rosendale, one that was so vibrant and alive. There was a period during the decline when there was hope for at least a modest revival. Because of its superior durability, the United States Public Roads Administration recommended that the concrete used in road construction contain a mix of about 20% natural cement. This allowed the last cement company in Rosendale to stay afloat for a few additional years. However, by 1970, the Century Cement Company (home of the Brooklyn Bridge cement) finally ceased operations.

As with a moth that lays its eggs and then fades away, so it was with Rosendale. However, before doing so, it initiated a chain of events which changed the complexion, character, and nature of the future development of the state of New York and its place in the history of the nation. Rosendale helped make possible the birth of the Delaware & Hudson Canal and was the primary factor responsible for its success.

The Delaware & Hudson Canal went on to bring millions of tons of coal to the state of New York. Finally, it was this coal which fueled the industrial revolution in New York, making it the Empire State of the nation.

The next chapter, The Water Wheel, may seem out of place in this book. However, the streams and rivers were the most important sources of power before the introduction of the steam engine and within their limits, played a significant part in the 19th Century industrial revolution.

CHAPTER XI

THE WATER WHEEL

Before going on into the age of the steam engine, the foundation upon which the industrial revolution was built, a pause should be taken to examine the role that the humble water wheel played in the economic development of the nation.

Except for an occasional windmill, the water wheel was the only source of non-human/animal power available in the nation before the advent of the steam engine. Until recently, the role of the water wheel in economic development has been marginallized and almost completely ignored. The water wheel was considered quaint, and at best, a suitable subject for aspiring artists. One of the purposes of this chapter is to try and restore some of this imbalance.

The water wheel played an essential role in the forming of our nation and in providing a secure foundation for the ensuing industrial revolution. In the early 19th Century, the United States was considered to be the largest user of water power in the world. As an example and in matters relating directly to this book, it was the construction of the giant water powered cement grinding mill at the Hudson River terminal of the D&H Canal, even before the canal's completion, that gave a jump start to the entire Rosendale cement industry.

Unlike England, which had one continuous industrial revolution, the United States had two industrial revolutions. The first was a mini-revolution, powered by the water wheel, beginning at the dawn of the 19th Century and continuing for about 50 to 60 years. The second was a large full scale industrial revolution, beginning in the middle of the mini-revolution and continuing into the 20th Century.

England's industrial revolution was almost entirely powered by steam. It began in earnest with the development and marketing of the first truly successful steam engine by James Watt (see Chapter XII). England had an abundant and accessible supply of coal, but only a limited supply of water power. In the United States, things were a little different. There was an abundant supply of both water power and coal. However, water power soon reached its limit. Coal, which initially was not accessible, became readily available during the era of the canals.

As late as 1800, 85% of the population of New York was still classified as rural. The major exception was the City of New York, which was classified as a merchant and trading center. Wealth was generally equated with the amount of land a person owned. The aristocrats of the time were the large land owners. There was an ever increasing number of affluent merchants in the city and to some extent in Albany. However, it was not until mid century that they became dominant in politics. Until then, the backbone of the state and the nation was still the self sufficient farm family.

The farm family raised or caught its own food and generally provided its own clothing, footwear, furniture, etc. The farmers traded for those items which they could not produce themselves, such as salt, sugar, wagons, harnesses, and cooking utensils. This lifestyle gave rise to the small rural village or town, which included a trading store, a blacksmith, a church, a mill, as well as some form of local militia. The purpose of the village was to service the farms within a radius of one or two days travel time. Almost by necessity, these communities were near a supply of water, i.e., streams, creeks, rivers, and lakes. The larger communities were located on the coast, or on bays and rivers flowing into the ocean.

At that time, the first requirement of almost any community was to find a millwright who could build a water powered mill, making use of the locally available water supply. Usually, the first mill to be built was the grist mill for the grinding of grain into flour. The only alternative to the grist mill was to grind grain Indian fashion. The Indians would put grain into a hollowed-out stone and then pound it with a heavy pole, which produced a meal, as opposed to flour.

Stories abound concerning the lengths to which a community would go in order to acquire the services of a millwright, who would build them a water powered grist mill. Land grants of 50 to 100 acres were not uncommon. Tales were told of fast talking millwrights, who would take ten to twenty years to build a grist mill. Some would never seem to finish and would continue to "milk" the community for years.

At that time, the building of a grist mill was more an art than a science. Estimates had to be made of the water flow, the quantity of water flowing, and the height of the fall of the water for each of the seasons of the year. The approximate "power" of the water had to be calculated so that the paddles could be designed, and the size, shape, and configuration of the wheel, gears, shafts, pulleys, and belts could be determined. These were all hand-made and hand fitted. The proper type of wood to be used was also an important determination. Finally, and most critical, the exact size, diameter, width, finish, and bore of the millstone had to be calculated. Any error or mismatch of any of these and the mill would not work properly, or maybe not at all.

Next in importance to the grist mill was the saw mill. Since the entire United States, east of the Mississippi River, was under a canopy of green trees, it made sense to build water powered saw mills. These mills produced the beams, planks, boards and shingles, which were needed for the building of houses, barns, shops, churches, sheds, etc. The finer woods were used for making furniture, while the blocks of other woods were split and used for fuel. Once these two mills were in place, then water power could be turned to industrial uses. Water wheels were used extensively in the tanning and paper industries. There were over 750 paper mills in the nation prior to 1850. Water wheels were used in the infant iron industry, especially for blowing, hammering, and rolling. The extraordinary use of water power in the textile industry is covered below.

The foregoing may seem of minor significance, but when taken in the aggregate, they become quite important. The following is a summary of the water powered mills operating only within New York state prior to the opening of the Erie Canal:

> Grist mills 2,140
> Saw mills 4,321
> Fulling mills (textiles) 993
> Carding mills (textiles) 1,235
> Tanneries .... 1,000 (+)
> Total .... 9,689 (+)

With a population of only about 1,372,800, this total would equate to one water powered mill for about every 142 people. The Village of Rosendale had water powered mills for grain, cement, textiles, and cider.

As with the industrial revolution in England and Europe, the mini-industrial revolution in the United States had its origins in the textile industry. At that time, there were four basic steps in the process of converting a bale of cotton, or wool, into finished cloth. The first step was carding, i.e., combing and straightening fibers. The next was the spinning of the fibers into thread or yarn. Then came the weaving of the thread/yarn into cloth, and finally there was the finishing (cleaning, printing, smoothing, etc.) of the cloth, making it ready for cutting and sewing.

Initially, all textile operations were done in the home or small work shop, employing all members of the family. The work was done on a piecemeal basis with the end product being the result of the efforts of the whole family and/or community. The final product was thus personalized, and the family or community became renowned for its quality, or lack thereof.

As a result of many inventions by a number of English mechanics and weavers, England became the world leader in the textile industry. Using the power of the steam engine, they were able to combine the four steps in textile production and place them in a single building, the forerunner of today's factory system. This, coupled with their new looms, flying shuttles, and jigs enabled England to out produce the rest of Europe. As a side light, it is interesting to note that this consolidation of the work force into factories caused a negative and violent reaction among the traditionalists in the textile industry. History records that many of these new factories were destroyed by the displaced home-centered textile tradesmen, who considered the factory to be a threat to their livelihood.

The advances that the English made in the textile industry were so great and so important that in 1781, they passed laws forbidding the export of textile technology. Not only was it forbidden to export textile machinery, drawings, etc., but individuals with detailed knowledge of textile machinery were forbidden to travel abroad.

It was in 1789, that a young gifted mechanic named Samuel Slater left England disguised as a farm laborer. He had secreted some drawings, but mostly, he had memorized the workings of textile machines. In 1790, he designed and built one of the first complete textile factories in the United States in Pawtucket, Rhode Island. It was powered by the water wheel. Although the mill was successful, it did not immediately blossom into the industrial revolution that some expected. There was a common belief, strongly promoted by the British, that cloth manufactured in England was better. It took the Embargo Act of 1807 and the War of 1812 to change people's minds. The Slater factory mysteriously caught fire (shades of England), while the owner was away. However, progress in the textile industry in the United Sates was not halted. The race to build water powered textile mills began with increased endeavor.

About the same time, in 1793, an American named Eli Whitney invented the cotton gin. It was a machine which automatically separated the seed from the cotton, previously a bottleneck in the processing of cotton. The cotton gin caused a veritable explosion in the growth of cotton in the United States. It transformed one-half of the nation's agricultural sector. See below:

1793: 1,500,000 lbs. cotton grown .... 15,000lbs. exported
1800: 35,000,000 lbs. cotton grown ...... 18,000,000lbs. exported

Although Eli Whitney invented the cotton gin, the rewards went to others who pirated his work. However, Eli Whitney went on to even greater fame. In 1799, he invented a new method of production referred to today as "mass production." He built a factory which produced 15,000 muskets in one year with all parts interchangeable. It was a process unheard of before. This was 100 years before Henry Ford. Later, the Eli Whitney factory in Connecticut evolved into the Winchester Repeating Arms Company.

Back to the War of 1812. With the embargo firmly in place, the United States was glutted with raw cotton. It was also about this time that another accomplished mechanic named Francis Cabot Lowell traveled throughout England and Europe, visiting all of the textile mills that he was permitted to see. He had a photographic memory and was able to retain most of what he saw. In 1813, he returned to the United States and set about building a complete textile mill/factory in Massachusetts. It was very successful, but the mill/factory soon ran out of water power.

Francis Lowell was not deterred. With strong financial backing from friends in Boston, he set about to once more revolutionize the textile industry. He selected the Merrimack River as his new site. Here, the powerful Merrimack River had a drop of about 28 feet in less than two miles. At this site, Lowell not only built a complete textile factory system, but an entire city as well. His workers came from the local under employed farm family members, mostly women and children. It was a utopian community, complete with churches, shops, schools, and parks. It was considered to be one of the industrial wonders of the world. Visitors from all over the world came to see and admire it. It was not long before it was producing 2,500,000 yards of cloth each week. It was all powered by water, interconnected by numerous canals, sluiceways, and conduits. The factories were equipped with an amazing array of shafts, pulleys, wheels, belts, and gears. Of course, the city was named in honor of its founder, Lowell, Massachusetts. However, even with this ideal location, it was not long before steam had to be introduced as a source of back-up power. In later years, steam became the primary source of power for the factory.

Lowell was not alone in this mini-revolution. Manchester was even larger. Lawrence specialized in woolen textiles. Lynn became the center for shoe manufacturing and all were powered by the water wheel. The Connecticut River was the second most industrialized river in New England. Most of the Connecticut products were of a mechanical nature: clocks, weapons, household items, farm utensils, and factory components. The factories themselves gave birth to new ancillary business sectors: wheels, shafts, gears, belts, pulleys, hinges, and bearings. One report during the mid 19th Century indicated that New England was using five times more waterpower per square mile than was being used by New York, New Jersey, and Pennsylvania combined.

Perhaps the most innovative advance during this mini-industrial revolution was at the managerial level. It was the new "corporate" system of ownership and management. About this time there were over 300 major corporations in the United States vs. only 20 similar corporations in England. The Delaware & Hudson Canal Company was one of the largest of such corporations.

Because of the abundance of water power in the United States, there was no immediate rush to convert to steam power as there was in England. There, coal was abundant, but water power was in limited supply. One of the advantages of water power was that the same water could be used repeatedly, sometimes as much as ten or twenty times. Initially, steam power was used as a back-up system to water power. However, with the rapid industrial expansion and the ever increasing need for greater productivity and mobility, the shortcomings of water power became apparent, and the conversion to steam power accelerated. Water power had its limitations, especially during periods of floods, droughts, and freezes. Probably the greatest limitation in the use of water power was not physical, but in the legalities attendant in its use. It was somewhat similar to the enormous quantity of product liability and class action suits clogging our legal system today.

During the mini-industrial revolution, the courts were jammed with litigation revolving around the question of "water rights." The first question that arose was whose "rights" had priority, especially during periods of scarcity. This question was especially ticklish where the same water was used by those further down stream and when a dam was involved. There was also the question of whether everyone needed the same quantity of water and during the same periods of time. There were rights of navigation to be considered. The lumber industry needed large quantities of water, almost on demand, to float their lumber down stream. Dams and diversions were unacceptable. Fishing rights were also a problem, especially when migratory fish were involved.

The farmers were probably the most vocal in their concern for their water rights. The most interesting concerned riparian rights. These involved everyone who owned property on the banks of a river. The owners downstream did not want their property to become a garbage dump for those who were up stream. At this time, rivers and streams were notoriously used for garbage and trash removal purposes. The list of water rights problems could go on and on, but simply stated, there was a log-jam of water rights cases in the courts of the day.

New England was the leader in the United States mini-industrial revolution. The Mid-Atlantic states, New York, New Jersey, and Pennsylvania played only a modest role in it. The southern and western states were virtual non-players. The major exceptions were the twin cities of Minneapolis and Saint Paul. They were founded at the cataract headwaters of the Mississippi River and used the turbulent waters there as a source of power for their industrialization.

In summary, it was the lowly water wheel, which powered the first mini- industrial revolution in the United States. As quaint as the water wheel may seem today, its importance in America's industrial revolution should not be underestimated. As a result, Boston became one of the most important business and financial centers in the nation. If it had continued for just a few more years, it is not beyond reason that the Statue of Liberty might have been placed in Boston Harbor. After all, it was one day's less sailing time to Europe.

Once the conversion to steam power began, there was no turning back. The Delaware & Hudson Canal was there to supply all of the coal that was needed. Before dismissing the water wheel, it is important to mention that use of the water wheel in the mini-industrial revolution resulted in the creation in the United States of one of the most advanced hydraulic engineering disciplines in the world. It developed the highly efficient water powered turbincs that are in use today.

It was this development that evolved into the mammoth hydro-electric plants of the 19th and 20th centuries, making the United States the premier industrial power of the world.

As explained above, the state of New York was not in the forefront of the water powered mini-industrial revolution, such as took place in New England. Its economy was agriculturally based, supported by an active and sophisticated mercantile sector. It did have an abundant supply of cheap coal, courtesy of the Delaware & Hudson Canal. With the advent of the steam engine and an endless supply of fuel, New York leaped directly into the industrial revolution, without having to supplant a water powered industrial base.

CHAPTER XII

STEAM POWER

PHASE I

One fact upon which all historians agree is that the steam engine powered the Industrial Revolution, which ushered in our modern age. Legend has it that James Watt, when he was a young boy, was fascinated by the power of steam. For hours at a time, he would watch the lid on a pot of boiling water in the fireplace. The steam from the boiling water would cause the lid to pop up and down. When he was older, he remembered the power of steam from the pot of boiling water, and so, he went out and invented the steam engine.

It's a nice story, but historical records seem to indicate otherwise. In fact, the steam engine can hardly be classified as having been invented. It really "evolved" over a period of almost 100 years before James Watt came onto the scene.

In the late 1600's, England's coal mines were experiencing a serious water seepage problem. The mines were being flooded with water, and they needed a means of pumping the water out of the mines. Many devices were tried, but with little success. About 1702, John Savery developed an atmospheric engine, which had a limited amount of success. However, many mines were too deep and beyond the limited capabilities of the Savery machine. John Savery went on to achieve everlasting fame, not because of his engine, but because he first used the term "horse power."

By 1712, Thomas Newcomen improved the Savery machine, and by 1760, they were being used successfully in many coal mines in England.

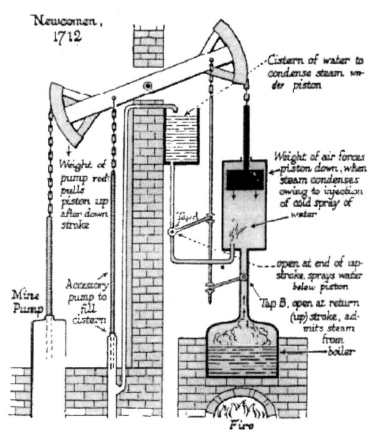

Courtesy: http://technolgy.niagarac.on.ca/people/mcsele/newcomen.htm
(origin unknown)

NEWCOMEN ATMOSPHERIC STEAM ENGINE

As with the Savery machine, the Newcomen machine was also an atmospheric machine. It was not steam power which "drove" the engine. The engine was "driven" by the power of the atmosphere. Steam would be introduced into a cylinder with an internal piston. Then a squirt of cool water would be sprayed into the steam filled cylinder. This would cause the steam to condense immediately to about 2/1000ths of its former volume, creating a vacuum. Then the atmospheric pressure outside of the cylinder would push the piston into the space (vacuum) created by the condensed steam. In other words, the "power" stroke of the piston was caused by the atmospheric pressure pushing down on the exposed side of the piston. This vertical action of the piston would move a rocker arm which, in turn, was attached to a shaft. The shaft went deep down into the mine and was connected to a pump, which pumped the water out of the mine. Initially, the opening and closing of the valves for steam and cool water was accomplished by a well coordinated individual. Although Savery's engine was often referred to as "the miner's friend," it was the Newcomen engine which was the most widely used.

It is a matter of record that Henry Ford discovered one of Newcomen's abandoned machines during a visit to England. He had the machine refurbished and brought it to the United States. It is still on exhibit in the Ford Museum in Dearborn, Michigan.

Courtesy; The Collections of The Henry Ford (P.O.19556)

**NEWCOMEN ATMOSPHERIC STEAM ENGINE
at the Henry Ford Museum**

Next on the scene was James Watt. He is called the "father" of the steam engine and, perhaps, rightly so. Whether he was ever fascinated by the popping up of the lid on a pot of boiling water is debatable. However, he was a gifted mechanic, and his services were much sought after. His biggest problem as a youth seemed to have been hiding from "press" gangs. They roamed London, trying to capture unattached youths for compulsory service aboard His Majesty's fighting ships.

He fled to Glasgow, where his services were in great need. He worked for the University of Glasgow and was charged with keeping its equipment in smooth running order. One day, he was asked to repair one of Newcomen's engines. This, he did, but after examining it, he was surprised to find that it was really a very simplistic device. He decided that he could improve on it and make it much more efficient. By 1776, he made a large number of improvements, which resulted in a quantum leap in the engine's performance. Some of them were as follows:

1. A separate condensing cylinder was added and insulated to prevent the loss of heat and power.
2. A mechanical governor was developed to open and close the valves more accurately.
3. Pistons were bored more precisely (as in the bore of a cannon) to prevent loss of power.
4. Lubricants (bear fat and tallow) were used to reduce friction and wear.
5. Steam "pressure" was added to the piston at the end of the power stroke to return it to its starting position. Although the steam pressure was low, 2-4 psi, it introduced the principle of a double acting piston, which could produce power going in both directions.
6. A vertical piston stroke was converted into a rotary flywheel motion, ideal for use in factories.

Another factor which helped make James Watt the true father of the steam engine was that he was an astute business person.

He was careful to protect his improvements with patents, and he entered into partnerships with wealthy and influential persons. Immediately, they set out to market and sell their engines for purposes other than to simply pump water out of coal mines. As early as 1783, they had convinced Richard Arkwright to use their steam engine to power his textile factory, which was the largest in England. They were so successful that by 1800, almost every textile factory in England was powered by a Watt's steam engine. They even sold one to Robert Fulton to power his steamboat, the *Clermont*.

As mentioned in the previous chapter, the United States lagged behind England in the use of steam engines to power factories. The reason was quite simple. There was little need for steam power for industrial use. The center for manufacturing in the United States was in New England, which was gifted with an abundant supply of natural water power. However, there was one use for steam power for which the United States had a great need and would shortly lead the world in its use for this purpose. This purpose was the use of steam power for water borne transportation.

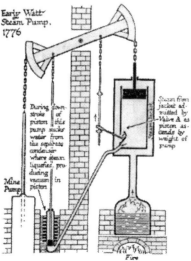

Courtesy: HTTP://technology.niagarac.om.ca/people/mcsele/newcomen.html

(origin unknown)
The first Watt Steam Engine

As with James Watt and the steam engine, the steamboat was not something that Robert Fulton thought of and developed by himself. The idea of using steam engines to propel boats was around for years. Attempts had been made in England, Europe, and even the United States long before Fulton's *Clermont*. Many credit John Fitch with building a successful steam powered boat in Philadelphia ten years before Fulton. Newspapers of the time confirm the fact. Not being as successful a promoter as Fulton, his boat soon faded from use and memory.

Robert Fulton spent years studying and experimenting with the problem of steam powered boats. Although one of his earlier boats sank when launched, he was not discouraged. He spent years studying such problems as how big the engine should be?; should the power take-off be by means of wheel or by vertical/horizontal shaft?; what size and shape should the paddle wheel be?; how large and at what angle should the slats be?; how big should the boat be?; and what shape and what draft should the boat have? He had to calculate the boat's resistance to water in order to attain a required speed of six miles per hour in still water. He had to estimate the boat's capacity for cargo and passengers in order to generate a profit. These are only some of the problems which Fulton had to study and solve. Not the least of his problems was that he had to find a boat builder who would build a boat to his exact specifications. Besides these technical problems, he was faced with a number of business related problems as well.

Similiar to James Watt, one of Fulton's first tasks was to protect all of his inventions and improvements with patents. Next, he had to find a suitable partner. Earlier while in Paris, Fulton met Robert Livingston, who was involved in negotiating the Louisiana Purchase with the French Government. He was one of the wealthiest and most influential men in the state of New York. It so happened that Livingston was so interested in steamboats that he had the New York legislature grant him a monopoly for all steam boat travel on the Hudson River. They made an ideal partnership. Of course, there was much litigation, but the monopoly lasted thirteen years. It was interesting to note that one of Fulton's fiercest legal opponents was a Colonel Ogden of New Jersey. However, after Fulton's untimely death in 1815, Ogden purchased Fulton's rights and then, just as fiercely, defended the monopoly against all others.

The case went all the way to the Supreme Court, and through a number of technical rulings by several courts, it was decided that states could not grant monopolies on navigable waterways. One factor which made this monopoly extremely attractive was that at the time New York claimed the entire Hudson River, including New York harbor, right up the New Jersey shoreline. It was illegal for New Jersey to launch a boat into the Hudson River or sail on it without the permission of New York. This, too, was a constant source of litigation. It was partially resolved in 1834, but not fully resolved until 1888 when it was agreed to divide the river right down the middle.

Back to Robert Fulton. His first successful steam boat trip took place on the Hudson River on his boat, later called the *Clermont*. The boat was reported to have been 133 feet long, 18 feet wide, had a draft of 7 feet, and was rated at 160 tons. Initially, it had 12 berths and could carry about 100 tons. Later, the cargo space was converted so that the boat could accommodate about 100 passengers. He used the James Watt steam engine for safety purposes. He was afraid that a high pressure boiler might explode.

On August 17, 1807, with much fanfare and some ridicule, the *Clermont* sailed from New York City, up the Hudson River, 150 miles to Albany. There was an intermediate stop for refreshments at Mr. Livingston's estate along the Hudson River at Clermont, NY. It made the trip to Albany in 32 hours and

S.W.Stant

Courtesy: Hudson River Maritime Museum, Kingston/Rondout, NY

ROBERT FULTON'S CLERMONT

the return trip to New York City in 30 hours. After this remarkable success, Robert Fulton hastily established regularly scheduled steamboat service all along the Hudson River between New York to Albany.

He then built a number of steamboats and expanded service around New York City and up Long Island Sound to New England. His boats included passenger packets, cargo carriers, tugs, and ferries. His ferry to New Jersey could carry 12 carriages, 30 horses, and as many as 300-400 passengers.

However, after the courts ruled that Fulton's monopoly was illegal, there was a veritable explosion of steamboat building and travel on the Hudson River. Some historians estimated that by mid-19th Century, there were more "steamboats" travelling on the Hudson River than on any other river in the world.

As could be expected, there were some steamboat races on the Hudson River, similar to the legendary days of the Mississippi River. Even the *Clermont* was challenged to a race. It ended in a no contest when the two boats collided. No severe damage was done and there were no injuries. To preclude any such mishaps in the future, the New York Legislature passed a law prohibiting such races. Steamboat captains, being steamboat captains, occasionally ignored the law, at times with serious consequences. In July, 1852, the *Henry Clay* challenged the *Arminia* to a race. The *Henry Clay*, by tying down the safety valve on its high pressure boiler, won the race. However, at the end of the race, in New York City, the two boats collided and a fire engulfed the *Henry Clay*. Despite being run aground, 72 passengers aboard the *Henry Clay* died.

Much of this chapter has been spent explaining the development of steamboat traffic on the Hudson River because this was a very important factor in the "industrial" development of the state of New York. However, to put it in proper perspective, it should be remembered that the *Clermont* sailed seven years before construction of the Erie Canal began. The decision to build the Erie Canal was long debated and closely contested. At one time, the decision to proceed with the construction was approved by only a single vote. The heavy volume of steamboat traffic on the Hudson River was probably the single most important factor used to tip the scales and gain approval for the canal.

The quantities and types of cargoes carried up, down, and between river ports were so great that it would be difficult to tabulate. Since this was before the era of the railroad, passenger travel by steamboat was not only heavy, but given priority. One estimate was that over 100,000 passengers traveled between Albany and New York City each year.

Perhaps, at this time, it would be appropriate to mention a new and innovative method, which was developed for transporting cargoes on the Hudson River using steamboats. It was the introduction of the steam powered "tugboat." Prior to the tugboat, all cargoes were carried aboard the boats themselves, whether powered by sail, paddles, oars, or steam. Now cargoes could be loaded onto canal or river barges, towed to their destinations, and left there to be loaded and/or unloaded, while the tugboat went on to tow other barges. Tugboats could tow many barges simultaneously. The basic principle is the same as what is being used on our highways today by the large tractor trucks and semi-trailers. Even passenger packet barges were towed up and down the Hudson River.

One interesting feature of the tugboat system was that canal barges could travel between canals and were not just limited to the canal of their origin. This was important to the industrial development of the state because in the 19th Century, New York had over 850 miles of canals. Walter Edmonds, the laureate of the Erie Canal, in his famous book *Rome Haul*, described how the less than clean D&H coal carrying canal barges would be derided when they traveled on the Erie Canal. There, they were in sharp contrast to the more tidy and pristine Erie Canal barges.

By the mid-19th Century, New York had an extensive network of canals, all connected to the Hudson River that bustling and dynamic highway of commerce. This network enabled millions of tons of cheap coal from Pennsylvania to be distributed to almost all sectors of the state, providing the power needed for its industrial revolution. With its transportation infrastructure in place and a plentiful and reliable source of inexpensive power, New York made a quantum leap into the industrial age. Its industrialization surpassed those of all other states, including those of New England. The following chapter will follow this theme, with special emphasis on a new type of steam engine, which was pioneered in the United States and was a key factor in New York's industrial revolution.

CHAPTER XIII

STEAM POWER

PHASE II

As mentioned in the previous chapter, Robert Fulton's steamboat was the precursor of the industrial revolution in the state of New York. In the meantime, interesting happenings concerning the steam engine were taking place in Pennsylvania. They were not going to sit by idly and watch New York usurp its leadership in the new nation.

During the early years of nationhood, Philadelphia considered itself to be the commercial and political center of the country. In 1800, it was the largest and most commercially active city in the nation. During this period, it was credited with having more sailings from its harbor on the Delaware River, than London had on the Thames River. Philadelphia tried to be the gateway to the West and was the biggest advocate of the ill-fated Mainline Canal, stretching from Philadelphia, all the way across the state to Pittsburgh.

The state of Pennsylvania was blessed with an enormous supply of natural resources. Literally, it was sitting on mountains of coal, both bituminous and anthracite. Since it lacked a viable internal transportation infrastructure, it sought other means of expanding its economic development. To its rescue came a small forge and foundry shop, the Oliver Evans & Sons Company. About the time that Robert Fulton was building his *Clermont*, Oliver Evans was experimenting with a different type of steam engine. The Watt's steam engine was too large, too immobile, and had an insatiable appetite for water. As such, it was not suitable for use in the interior of Pennsylvania.

The Evans' steam engine overcame all of these shortcomings. It was so successful that it changed the design of all future steam engines. The downside was that it nudged the economic development of the state of Pennsylvania in a direction that was not intended. Instead of becoming a major commercial and trading center, it became the center for the nation's heavy industry. As such, it not only became the "Keystone" state, but also the "smokestack" state as well.

Oliver Evans was an ingenious mechanic who built steam engines and tinkered with the whole concept of what made steam engines run. He reasoned: why not let the "expansive" power of steam in an engine do the work instead of the "condensing" power of steam, as in the Watt engine? As mentioned earlier, steam when condensed back to water, reduced its volume by about 500 times, creating a vacuum, commonly referred to as "condensing" power. Correlatively, when water is boiled, it creates an equal amount of "expansive" power, which could be further increased 2,3,4,5 or more times, depending upon the amount of steam pressure in the boiler. In other words, the "condensing" power of steam could not be increased, but the "expansion" power of steam could be increased. Evans further reasoned that if successful, the benefits would be enormous. Efficiency would be increased. Much less fuel and water would be required. The weight of the engine would be reduced significantly. Most important, there would be a tremendous increase in the mobility of the engine. They could be moved easily and set up almost anywhere, making their use ideal for the coming industrial revolution.

Although the theory and capability of the expansion-type steam engine was well known, it was not put into use because of fear that excessive high pressure would cause the engine to explode. All of Watt's engines were of the condensing type. This was the reason all of Fulton's steamboats used the Watt's-type engine. Their fears were justified, as will be noted later.

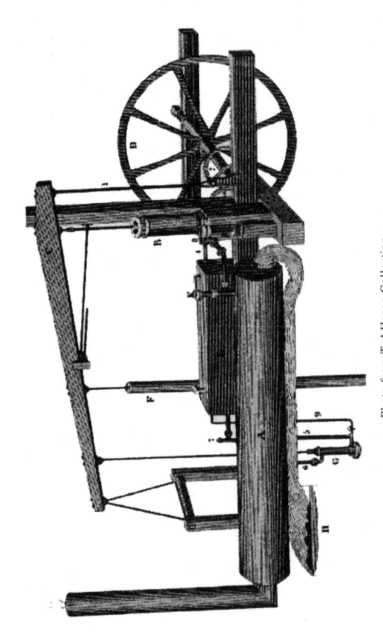

Photo from Ted Hazen Collection

Oliver Evans' Columbian Steam Engine

Despite its wide use, the condensing engine had a number of disadvantages. They were very heavy, some over 100 tons. The condenser required large amounts of water – about 20 gallons per minute. This was 20-30 times the quantity of water required for an expansion-type engine. Having a vertical cylinder/piston, it had a high center of gravity and was less efficient than a cylinder in the horizontal position. Being inefficient, it required enormous quantities of fuel. It is estimated that before coal was introduced on the Hudson River, the Watt steam powered boats consumed about 200,000 cords of wood during the normal 8-10 month period when the river was free of ice.

Oliver Evans was experimenting with non-condensing, or expansion type engines at about the same time Fulton was building the *Clermont*. Being a gifted mechanic, Evans was able to build boilers and piston cylinders that could safely handle pressures of 40-50 pounds per square inch (psi). Watt's steam engine used only 2-4 pounds per square inch of pressure. This low pressure was used only to return the piston to its starting position, so that the condensing action of the steam could begin its power stroke. In contrast, Evans used the expansive power of steam to provide the power stroke of the engine. This eliminated the condensing cylinder, the water reservoir for the condensing cylinder, and all of the associated control equipment, reducing the engine's weight by about one-third. He also placed the power cylinder in a horizontal position, providing greater stability, further reducing weight and increasing efficiency. Evans created a more mobile type of steam engine, which could be placed anywhere, independent of a large water supply, making it perfect for use in the emerging industrial revolution.

Since Pennsylvania was literally sitting on mountains of coal, the expansion-type steam engine was immediately put into use all over the state in mines, foundries, and in iron and steel mills. This gave the state a great lead in the creation of heavy industries. According to some historians, by the 1850's, the

United States could compete successfully with England in coal, iron, and steel.

With the successful introduction of the non-condensing, or expansion-type steam engine, it was not long before a sliding, or shuttle valve was developed. Now, high power steam pressure could be applied to both sides of a free floating piston. This resulted in the engine having a power stroke going in both directions, further increasing its efficiency. Later, the most visible application of this principle was in the pistons, which drove the old steam powered railroad locomotives.

Another factor, which gave the Evans' expansion engine a boost, was its almost universal use on the Mississippi River and its tributaries. Unlike the deep Hudson River with high palisades, these waterways were shallow, had low sloping banks, and were filled with shifting sandbars. Except for the lower Mississippi and the New Orleans area, the deep draft (7+ feet) boats using the heavy Watt engines were not suitable for use on these waterways. This was especially so because the boats using the Mississippi River network seldom had city piers or docks to tie up to. Rather, they had to run up onto the shallow river banks to load and discharge their passengers and cargoes.

As early as 1811, steamboats were being built in Pittsburgh with the new lighter weight expansion-type steam engine and began traveling up and down the Ohio and Mississippi Rivers. These boats had only half the draft of the Fulton boats and soon dominated steamboat travel on the interior waterways of the nation, giving us one of the most colorful periods in our nation's history. Records indicate that during the 1840's, there were about 1,000 steam powered riverboats traveling on our nation's inland waterways.

Of course, this came with costs. The danger of explosions using high pressure expansion engines was well documented. According to a survey taken by the United States government in 1832, there had been 380 riverboat explosions using expansion-type steam engines. These explosions resulted in 865 fatalities. There had been only 18 riverboat explorations with 9 fatalities when using condensing-type steam engines. The three basic reasons for the disproportionate number of explosions of the expansion-type engines could be summarized as follows:

1. Captains wanting more power often had the safety valves on the boilers tied down.
2. The stokers tending the boilers were usually the lowest paid and least qualified members of the crew.
3. Initially, the engines and especially the boilers were of poor quality.

During this period, there were no large and well equipped engine and boiler factories. The engines were built in small foundries and forging shops, which employed less than 20 employees and produced only 1-10 units a year.

Once the Delaware & Hudson Canal began bringing massive amounts of coal into the state and the expansion-type engines proved their worth, New York began its unprecedented industrial revolution. The fact that these boilers and engines could be manufactured in small foundries, forges, and even in blacksmith shops, helped a great deal. There were over a thousand of these shops in the state. By the mid-19th Century, there were more steam engines in New York state than any other state. It is interesting to note that in the later half of the 19th Century, one of the largest steam engine factories in the nation was located in Brooklyn.

Many improvements evolved during the 19th Century to increase the efficiency and to reduce, even further, the size and weight of the expansion-type steam engine. Frederick Sickels and George Corliss developed a complicated automatic cut-off valve control system that increased the efficiency of the engine. In their system, the intake of high pressure steam was regulated by the length of travel of the piston in the cylinder of the engine. The supply of high pressure steam was cut off sharply, after the piston had traveled only one-tenth of its normal length of travel. They let the "expansive" power of the steam push the piston the remaining nine-tenths. It was a tremendous fuel saver, by a factor of three. The story is told of one factory owner, who, at the time of purchase, balked at paying the high cost of the new engine. Instead, he opted to pay only a percentage of the cost of the fuel saved over a two-year period. It turned out that after two years, he paid twice as much as the original cost of the engine.

Probably the most popular "non-condensing" steam engine, which was used in New York's industrial revolution, was the Baxter engine. It was small, compact, and required floor space measuring only four feet square. It could fit into almost any basement and was ideally suited for the thousands of small factories and shops located in urban areas.

At this point, a few words should be added about steam boilers, the stepchild of the steam engine. They were always under-appreciated and until mid-19th Century, did not undergo much improvement. The early boilers of The Newcomen era were shaped like giant kettles with a copper dome, similar to the copper kettles used to make beer. In fact, that's what they were patterned after. James Watt, along with his other improvements, built a better boiler. It resembled a giant coffin, which was used as a fire bed. Over the fire bed was placed a long cylinder, containing the water that was to be boiled. Later, Watt placed a flue (12 inch diameter exhaust pipe) through the water in the cylinder, from one end through to the other end. The hot exhaust from the burning coals in the fire bed was passed through the flue and on up the chimney. In this manner, the same heat from the burning coals was used twice to heat the water.

The early boilers were not renown for their quality. The water and high pressure steam were contained in long, large diameter cylinders. They were manufactured by assembling curved iron plates and bolting them together with rivets. As with the firemen who attended the boilers on steamboats, the rivet pounders and aligners were the least paid and least qualified workers in the foundry. As a result, many boilers contained flaws and had a tendency to explode when under high pressure. The United States Census Bureau recorded that during one twelve year period, there were about 1,300 boiler explosions in factories with over 2,500 fatalities. Besides improved manufacturing techniques, outside factors entered onto the scene to help correct the situation. They were in the form of government and insurance company inspectors.

Finally, towards the end of the 19th Century, improvements were made in the design of boilers. The first was that instead of one large diameter flue, carrying hot exhaust gases through the water as in the Watt's boiler, the exhaust gases were passed through many small diameter pipes. This almost doubled the efficiency of the boiler. There was one final improvement which is still with us today. Instead of passing the hot exhaust gases through the small diameter tubes in the boiler, water was passed through the tubes. Then the tubes were placed just above the hot coals in the boiler fire bed.

It must be mentioned that England was not sitting idly by and letting the United States assume the world leadership in the development, manufacture, and use of steam engines. Led by Richard Trevithick, they also developed non-condensing, expansion-type steam engines. However, the British were wedded to the Watt condensing-type of steam engine, and in addition, they lacked the dynamics of the American industrial revolution. As a result, the United States became the world's leader in the development, manufacture, and use of steam engines. The British did manage to surpass the United States in one specialized field. It was in the use of steam engines to propel ocean-going vessels. They had an immense empire and had to find a better way of uniting it. Sailing vessels were too slow, and the existing steam engines required too much fuel for long ocean voyages. The British developed a "compound" type of steam engine, which used the same steam a number of times. Once they discovered how to safely use ocean water in their steam engine, they even incorporated a "condensing" cycle into their "compound" engine, further increasing its efficiency.

In addition to factory and steamboat use, the United States also led the world in the development and use of steam to power railroad locomotives. So much has been written about the subject that it will not be examined in this book. After the canal era railroads completed the task of uniting the nation. The railroads not only expanded the nation's industrial revolution, especially during the 20th Century, but gave it a westward orientation as well. The emergence of the "expansion" type of steam engine was a key element in this development.

The early locomotives were too weak to climb hills, even those with a moderate slope. Their design made them unable to negotiate sharp turns. Originally, they were suitable only for passenger travel and for hauling small, lightweight express-type packages. In fact, the early sponsors of the railroads were the canal companies. They wanted to reduce their passenger traffic, so they could concentrate on the more profitable freight traffic. However, once the expansion-type steam engine proved its worth, the nation's craze for railroad construction expanded dramatically. During one ten year period, New York state alone granted 106 charters for new railroads. By the end of the Civil War, there were over 30,000 miles of railroad track in the country. As with the Mississippi River steamboats, the railroads left a pronounced and lasting legacy for the nation.

There was one additional field in which the United States led the world in the application and use of steam power. It was in the use of steam power to provide fresh water for the new metropolitan areas springing up all over the country. The older countries of the world had centuries within which to develop their water systems. The United States did not have that luxury. The new cities needed water immediately. The steam driven water pump came to the rescue. By the late 19th Century, there were over 1,000 cities which used steam power to supply their fresh water needs. The most famous (or notorious) example was the city of Philadelphia. These steam powered water pumps were enormous in size, many weighting well over 100 tons and standing over 100 feet tall.

New York state was fortunate in that most of its cities had gravity fed water systems, the most famous was the Croton Reservoir water system for New York City. The reservoir was 41 miles from the city and was connected to the city by cement-lined aqueducts and tunnels. It was built with Rosendale cement and by John Jervis of Delaware & Hudson Canal fame. To this day, New York is considered to have one of the best supplies of fresh water of any megalopolis in the world.

By the middle of the 19th Century, the industrial revolution had blossomed in New York state. Because of all of the preceding factors, it was being propelled into its role as the Empire State of the nation. New York's two main competitors were Massachusetts and Pennsylvania. Massachusetts was wedded to the water wheel, had reached its plateau, and could progress no further. Pennsylvania, because of its severe topographical problems, drifted into its role as the United States center for heavy industry. It might have competed successfully with New York if it had been able to establish a viable east-west waterway to the western territories. Despite the fact that the state had more steam engines than all of France, they were not helped by the fact that two of their busy waterways, the West Branch Canal and the Susquehanna River, flowed into the Chesapeake Bay, much to the delight of Baltimore.

In summary, it was the availability of the expansion-type steam engine, fueled by the millions of tons of cheap coal carried by the Delaware & Hudson Canal that propelled New York into the industrial age. This theme will be developed further in subsequent chapters.

CHAPTER XIV

INDUSTRIAL DEVELOPMENT

GENERAL

The principles of industrial development can be compared to a three-legged stool. If one leg is absent, the stool would not be able to stand and would fall over and collapse. For purposes of this book, we will call one leg "people," the second leg, "transportation infrastructure," and the third leg, "power." Some proponents of industrial development insist that there is a fourth leg, "an adequate supply of potable water." It is an important factor, but since most cities in the United States were almost equally endowed, it was not considered as one of the controlling factors of America's 19th Century industrial development.

Today, there are many additional factors to be considered in industrial development. These include friendly governmental attitude, environmental impact, supportive financial institutions, adequate supply of raw materials, accessibility to potential markets, etc. Important as these factors are, they are flexible, mobile in nature, and corrective action can be taken should the need arise. When considering the 19th Century industrial development of the nation, these factors are not in the same category as those of the three-legged stool cited previously.

The first leg of the industrial development stool, "people", was critical in the United States, but was considered less critical in Europe. There, all of the people needed were already in place and increasing in numbers each year. Also, they possessed an inherent technical orientation. In Europe, they had the luxury of time. Their industrial development spanned a couple of centuries, while in the United States the development was compressed into decades.

A prime example of the importance of the "people" factor can be found in the history of the state of California. For almost one hundred years, it bumbled along with negligible industrial development. The glaring missing factor needed for industrialization was "people," It wasn't until the mass migration of people into California during the 20th Century that California became the industrial giant that it is today.

The "people" factor when applied to the eastern states was quite unique in the history of industrial development. It did not take place during a single period but was stretched over several centuries and reached its peak in the 19th Century. This development consisted of three distinct waves of immigration.

The first wave of settlers could be classified as religious refugees. They were the Pilgrims of Massachusetts, the French Huguenots of New York, the Catholics of Maryland, and the Quakers of Pennsylvania. They came with their families to find a place where they could live in harmony with their beliefs. They were equally at home working on their farms, sailing on the seas, or working at their trades.

The second wave of settlers were the peasants of Europe. They owned little or nothing. Most had worked as serfs longing for the day when they could own their own farms, till their own soil, and raise a family without being beholden to a lord or landlord. Included in this group were tens of thousands of indentured servants, who were brought over to the new land and were obligated to toil for a master for a certain number of years. When the opportunity presented itself, they moved to the interior and started a new and independent life for themselves. Both groups of the second wave had a tendency to become farmers, adding strength to the backbone of the nation. They built the houses they lived in, raised the food they ate, and made the clothes they wore. They needed little help from others, or from the government, and united mostly for self defense.

The third wave of immigrants was slightly different. They were mostly economic refugees, who came to the United States for a better life. They wanted to escape the economic hardships and repressions of their homeland. Perhaps, the most notable were the Irish, who were also fleeing the potato famine at home. Others, mostly from central Europe were escaping the harsh political realities and economic conditions of their homelands. After all, "The streets in America were paved with gold," or so the stories went. They were different from their predecessors in that they seldom came with their families. Many sent for them later, and some went back to their homeland to find a bride and bring her to the "promised land."

When single men first came to the United States, they were looking for employment as opposed to owning farms. As a result, they gravitated to the mines, to large construction projects, to iron and steel mills, and to the numerous factories, which were springing up in all of the urban areas. It was this last factor which facilitated the unprecedented industrial development of the nation. Stories abound about how single men were recruited right off the immigration docks and hustled off to factories in cities all over the eastern part of the nation. Those that weren't so recruited, tended to congregate in urban areas forming little communities of their own. This enabled them to become the predominant labor force for whatever industry happened to be in the area. The Jews in the garment industry of New York City and the Poles in the tin can industry of Jersey City were typical examples. They were the source of the "people" leg of the industrial development stool.

According to most historians, urbanization was the essential element in the industrialization of America in the 19th Century. As prominent and as note worthy as were the textile mills and other water powered factories in New England, in the aggregate, they only comprised about 10% to 12% of the nation's gross industrial product at the end of the 19th Century. Even when coupled with the heavy industries of Pennsylvania, they still comprised less than 25% of the nation's gross industrial product. It was the thousands upon thousands of small and medium sized factories, springing up almost simultaneously in all of the urban areas of the country which accounted for the remaining 65% to 75% of the nation's gross industrial production. These new urban areas transcended the rural self-sufficient communities, which the founding fathers had in mind.

The second leg of the industrial development stool, was a viable "transportation infrastructure." This has been a major development factor since the dawn of civilization. History records that cities and commercial centers invariably arose at junctures of transportation routes. These junctures could be seaports, river junctions, mountain passes, caravan trail crossings, etc. Damascus, in the middle of nowhere, became a thriving trading center because caravan trails met there. The Roman Empire had command of the sea-lanes, and also one of the most extensive road systems ever built (over 100,000 miles). There is an old saying, "All roads lead to Rome." Constantinople was one of the most important cities of the ancient and medieval worlds because it was located on the Bosporus Straits.

Availability of transportation routes continued to be a key to national power long after the fall of Rome. Until late in the middle ages, this usually meant that a center of power had to be located on the sea or to have easy access to the sea. The empires of the Vikings, Spanish, British, and even to the modest empires of such small countries as Holland and Portugal were founded upon this principle. When the industrial age began, not only was there a requirement to move great quantities of goods and material worldwide, but to inland destinations as well. To solve the problem of inland movement, networks of canals were built. Later, the canals were replaced by railroads. This continued into the 20th Century when highways became the dominant means of inland transportation.

Finally, the airplane became an important means of transportation, both nationally and internationally. A prime example of this evolution is Miami which was transformed from a tourist trap into the commercial and financial center of the Americas. The reason is that Miami is the closest aerial embarkation port in the United States to all of South America, Central America, the Caribbean, and even southern Mexico.

In colonial times, a viable transportation system was considered so essential that all cities of any significance were located either on the ocean or had easy access to the ocean. The cities of Boston, New York, Philadelphia, Baltimore, and Charleston were notable examples. As a footnote in history, one of the reasons that our nation's capital was located on the Potomac River was because of its access to the ocean. It was located as far up the river as possible, near the cataracts of Great Falls. The original grant for Washington, D.C. included Arlington County, Virginia. In 1846, Arlington was ceded back to Virginia under the false belief that it was in excess to the needs of the nation's capital.

About that time, nearby Alexandria was an important seaport. It handled one of our nation's most profitable exports, i.e. tobacco. In fact, a "hogshead of tobacco" was used as a form of currency. George Washington, until the day he died, tried to extend the Chesapeake & Ohio Canal from Washington, D.C., all the way to the Ohio River so that the capital of the nation would be the Gateway to the West. An aqueduct (Key Bridge) was built from the District to Virginia so that barges could float across the Potomac to the port of Alexandria. Once a transportation infrastructure was in place, it was envisioned that the capital, together with Alexandria, would become a major commercial center, as well as the nation's capital.

During the 19th Century, there were numerous examples of business and commercial centers springing up all over the nation because they were located at transportation junctures. Pittsburgh was located where the Allegheny and Monongahela Rivers join to form the Ohio River. Kansas City was so located because someone decided to build a railroad bridge across the Missouri River there. El Paso was located at a pass through the mountains. Chicago became the link between the Mississippi River and Lake Michigan. In the railroad era, because it was at the southern tip of Lake Michigan, it became the rail center of the nation. To go from New York to San Francisco one had to change trains at Chicago.

Not only nationally, but internationally as well, a viable transportation infrastructure is considered essential for economic development. The US Agency for International Development believes it to be of such prime importance to all developing nations that it is placed on the priority list for all of its assistance programs. They too consider it to be one of the essential legs of the economic development stool.

The third leg of the industrial development stool is "power." In order to achieve industrialization, it is necessary to have a source of abundant, reliable, and cheap power.

In earlier civilizations and for thousands of years afterwards, power was limited to human power and animal power. Even the Bible makes reference to this type of power when it advised not to muzzle an ox, while it is rotating an ancient gristmill. Over the years, man enhanced the capability of these sources of power with such devices as the wheel, lever, inclined plane, pulley, and screw. It is amazing what monumental structures, such as the pyramids, the acropolis, and coliseums were built using only human/animal power, enhanced by these simple devices.

Human/animal power reached its peak during the Roman Empire, and there were no major advances for almost a thousand years. There were outstanding castles, cathedrals, and cities built during that period, but there was little or no technological advancement made in developing new sources of "power."

However, during this thousand year period, some advances were made in the use of "wind" power. Probably, the most notable success was in the use of "wind" power to move ships at sea. On land, the Low Countries made excellent use of "wind" power in the form of windmills to grind their grain. Both were reasonably successful, but still there was little technological advancement.

This 1000 year technological drought came to an end in the 18th century with the introduction of "steam" power into the world's economy. It was the British who pioneered the use of steam power. It was their use of steam power in their factories that began the world's industrial revolution. England was fortunate in that they had an enormous supply of coal to provide all of the fuel they needed to generate their steam power.

It was the application of steam power that propelled England into the industrial age and gave them the vital third leg of the industrial development stool. They already had the first leg "people", since their country was relatively densely populated. If more workers were needed, they simply obtained them from Ireland or one of their many colonies. They also had the second leg, a viable transportation infrastructure. England had a well developed road system. Also, they had one of the best canal systems in Europe. Since they commanded the seas, there was no problem with external transportation needs. Their transportation infrastructure enabled them to import raw materials for their factories and then export finished products to their customers, worldwide.

In the United States, there was a delayed reaction to England's industrial revolution. It did not start here until 20-30 years after it began in England and did not really get into full swing until 40-50 years after England. The basic reason was that, initially, the new nation had none of the three legs of the industrial development stool.

The first leg, people, was lacking until the third wave of immigration took place. As an example, New York was ranked seventh in terms of population when the nation was founded. Besides, those who were already in the country were more interested in farming than in working in factories.

The second leg, a viable transportation infrastructure was not in place. At the time, it was limited to the ocean, bays, and navigable streams and rivers. It did not become a reality until the era of canals and steamboats.

The third leg, power was also lacking. When the nation was founded, coal was being imported from England. Apparently, the entrepreneurs of New England were the only ones interested in industrial development. They were fortunate in that there were many streams and rivers to give them a limited source of power, sufficient for them to begin their mini-industrial revolution.

As noted above, in order for a full fledged industrial revolution to take place, all three legs of the industrial development stool had to be in place. This chapter discussed industrial development in general terms. The following chapter will apply the principles of the three legged stool more definitively to 19th Century America.

CHAPTER XV

INDUSTRIAL DEVELOPMENT

USA

During the 19th Century, the United States changed from an inconsequential former colony populated by tillers of the soil into one of the greatest industrialized nations of the world. It was a feat unparalleled in all human history. It was in this unprecedented industrial development that the state of New York played a dominant roll, and it was Rosendale that provided the foundation for New York to assume that position.

Industrial development in the United States began in the New England area in the early 19th Century. Up until the War of 1812, there was little need for industrialization in the new nation. What the self-sufficient farm families could not produce for themselves, was imported from Europe. They imported iron kettles for their fireplaces, fine furniture and dinnerware for their homes, textile goods for themselves, and coal and cement for their industrial needs.

The cities such as Boston, New York, and Philadelphia were really trading centers, where goods and products were bought, sold, and traded. The thriving fishing and whaling businesses also fell into this general category. The remainder of the country was agriculturally oriented. They produced a wide variety of items, such as grains, vegetables, meats, and dairy products, as well as cotton, wool, leather, lumber, and furs.

It took the War of 1812 to change the thinking of many people. A consensus was formed among the people which believed that the nation should be more self-sufficient. They felt that the country should increase its manufacturing capabilities and should be less reliant on Europe. A number of societies and groups were formed to promote various types of manufacturing, with the aim of making the nation more industrially independent. Laws were passed to benefit new industries and the theme, "Private gain for public good," was in vogue. It might be noted that one of the earliest leaders of this movement, well before the War of 1812, was Alexander Hamilton.

At that time, New England was considered to be the nation's leader in entrepreneurship. The term "Yankee Trader" had some basis in fact. Some say that it began with the infamous "Triangular Trade" (rum, sugar, and slaves). Others postulate that it began with their prosperous fishing fleets, especially their whaling fleets. While some believe that it originated with the puritanical concept that idleness was equated with sinfulness. Regardless of its origin, industrialization in the United States began in New England. By European standards, it was classified only as a mini-industrial revolution. In order to become a full scale industrial revolution, New England had to possess all three legs of the industrial development stool: people, a viable transportation infrastructure, and an abundant, cheap, and reliable source of power.

The people leg of the development stool was not too difficult to assemble. By colonial standards, New England was relatively densely populated. The initial work force came from the surrounding farm communities. The farm family tended to be quite large, such as the Snyder family cited in Chapter III. Although the farm family was very busy during the planting and harvesting, there was a surplus of labor during other periods. This was especially so for the female members of the farm family. They welcomed the opportunity for outside employment and for the chance to earn "hard" money.

The early manufacturers went to great lengths to make their workers comfortable and well cared for, even to seeing to their religious needs. The early factory sites could almost be classified as small utopian communities, with adequate housing and numerous community services. However, as time wore on, things began to change, especially when down turns in the market place caused economies in the work place. Despite these problems, industrial development progressed without too many upheavals. When more workers were needed, there was a ready supply from Europe, especially from Ireland, England, and France.

The second leg of the development stool, transportation infrastructure, was acceptable, but barely so. New England had a decent north-south capability, but a poor east–west capability. Their streams and rivers also had a north-south orientation. To compensate for their poor transportation capabilities, they built a number of canals.

Twenty years before the Erie Canal, they built the successful Middlesex Canal to connect the textile mills along the Merrimack River to the port of Boston. Connecticut built the New Haven & Northhampton Canal, and Rhode Island built the Blackstone Canal. Maine built the special purpose (forest products) Cumberland & Oxford Canal. Boston even seriously considered building a canal across the state to connect with the Hudson River and the Erie Canal, in the hopes that it would become the nation's doorway to the West.

As concerns the third leg of the development stool, "power," New England was blessed with quite a few streams, rivers, and waterways. These not only contained large amounts of water, but had significant drops of elevation along their routes, which permitted them to be harnessed to generate power for their industries. Seizing the opportunity, New Englanders built factories along these waterways and powered them with that ancient device called the waterwheel. Textile mills were built in Lowell and Manchester. Shoe factories were built in Lynn. Clock and weapons' factories were built in Connecticut. Rhode Island built steam engines and boilers. This cheap and available source of power allowed New England to begin its mini-industrial revolution early in the 19th Century.

New England continued to expand its mini-industrial revolution until one of the legs of the industrial development stool reached its absolute limit. It was the "power" leg of the stool, which had reached its limit. As explained in Chapter XI, waterpower had specific limits. It was not 100% reliable, especially during freezes, floods, and droughts. New England tried to remedy these problems by supplementing their waterpower with steam power. There was a plentiful supply of wood, which could be used as fuel for their steam boilers. However, as more and more wood was being used, it became less plentiful and more expensive. They tried to use coal to replace the wood, but it too became more expensive.

Coal had to be shipped via sailing vessel from Philadelphia. The only other source was coal from New York, which came via the Delaware & Hudson Canal. Since the delivery of coal to New York factories would be less expensive than coal delivered to New England factories, it meant that New York factories would enjoy a competitive edge. It also meant that in case of shortages, New York would have priority on the use of what coal was available.

With no other acceptable substitute for coal in the 19th Century to fuel its industrial expansion, New England's industrial base began to wither. It tried to extend the life of its industries during the railroad era, but was unable to regain its competitive edge. Today, New England is more renown for its ivy-covered institutions of higher learning than for any of its industrial products, except perhaps the colt revolver.

As for the rest of the nation, industrial growth during the 19th Century ranged from negligible to unprecedented.

The southern states were wedded to agriculture. There was some industrial development around Atlanta, Charleston, and Richmond, but most of the products were for the local markets. Very few of the non-agricultural products were for export or nationwide use.

The Midwest did not achieve its industrial boom until late in the 19th Century and early 20th Century. It had to wait for the railroad era to provide the necessary second leg, transportation infrastructure, of the industrial development stool. The people leg of the stool was also weak until the middle and latter half of the 19th Century. As dramatic as the later developments were, they are not pertinent to the issues raised in the book and will not be examined further.

It was in the Mid-Atlantic States (Pennsylvania, New Jersey, Delaware, and New York) where the greatest industrial development took place during the 19th Century. It set a pattern, which continued well into the 20th Century.

Unlike New England, Pennsylvania was fortunate in that it had an inexhaustible supply of cheap fuel to power its industrial development, leg # 3. It was sitting upon mountains of coal, enough to fuel its industries for centuries. It was also fortunate in that it had a sufficient number of "people," leg #1 of the industrial development stool to fulfill its industrial needs. It should be remembered that for almost the first fifty years, Philadelphia was the largest city in the nation.

What Pennsylvania did not have was a viable transportation infrastructure, leg # 3 of the industrial developmental stool. The problem was that the Appalachian Mountain range crossed the state in a north-south direction, making east-west travel very difficult. It tried valiantly to overcome this deficiency by every means at its disposal. It built canals, over 900 miles of them, turnpikes, roads, tunnels, and even a 38 mile portage railroad. The state literally spent itself into insolvency.

Despite their limited east-west transportation capability, they did quite well with what they had. In the West, Pittsburgh became famous for its iron and steel industry. Sadly, the use of locally available bituminous (soft) coal, did not enhance the environment. As early as 1811, Pittsburgh Boat Builders began building shallow draft steamboats, ideal for the Ohio and Mississippi Rivers. Just in time for the Civil War, they manufactured large quantities of steel rails, steam locomotives, and cannons. The renown Pittsburgh Plate Glass (PPG) Company was located there. After the discovery of oil in Titusville, 1859, it became the first oil distribution center in the nation.

In the East, Philadelphia considered itself to be the leading city in the country during the early days of nationhood. Besides being the largest, it was the nation's capital until 1800. Robert Morris, who was credited with financing the American Revolution, established the nation's first charter bank in Philadelphia. Because it was adjacent to the anthracite coal fields and had three short canals connecting it to them, it became one of the major coal distribution centers for the coal industry. It was also a major shipbuilding center and together with its New England counterparts, was building about 1/3 of all British merchant sailing ships. Until eclipsed by New York, it was the nation's leading business, financial, and trading center.

It was not until the latter part of the 19th Century, when the full impact of the railroad made itself felt, that Pennsylvania was able to overcome its initial lack of a viable transportation infrastructure. However, by that time Pennsylvania had drifted into the heavy industry business sector and had to be satisfied with being number two in industrial development.

New Jersey, being located between Philadelphia and New York, had the necessary "people" to fulfill the requirements of the first leg of the development stool. Also, being next to the enormous coal deposits in Pennsylvania, it had access to all of the coal needed to power industrial expansion, giving it the third leg of the stool. Despite few natural barriers, New Jersey had only a limited transportation infrastructure. Its two main waterways were the Delaware River and the Hudson River. Unfortunately, both rivers were on the borders of the state, so that benefits derived from the rivers had to be shared with its neighboring states. Also, the Hudson River and the harbor of New York in its entirety, were claimed by the state of New York. This severely hampered New Jersey's industrial development until the claim was finally settled in the latter part of the 19th Century. It was then that New Jersey also began to enjoy the full benefits of a robust international trade.

Similar to its neighbors, New Jersey tried to overcome its deficiency in transportation by building canals. It built two cross state canals, the Morris and the Delaware and Raritan Canals. Unfortunately, the principle cargoes carried over one of the canals were of the "pass through" variety, which benefited its neighboring states as much as, if not more so, than New Jersey itself. Further, it might be mentioned that the other canal was so mismanaged that at times it was more of a liability than an asset.

New Jersey had a unique pattern of development. Initially, it had a respectable industrial base, iron forges and foundries, factories for glass and leather products, and textile mills. It was Alexander Hamilton who helped establish Paterson, the perfect factory town. It used the 77 foot drop in the Passaic River at Great Falls to power its factories, which produced textiles (especially silks), firearms, and later, even railroad locomotives. Colonel John Stevens, inventor of the screw propeller for boats, had his ship building facilities around Newark.

New Jersey's gentle rolling terrain and the fact that it was located between the two largest cities in the nation, resulted in its becoming the bread basket for both metropolitan areas. It was so successful that it adopted "Garden State" as its motto. Later, vegetable canning became one of its most important industries.

In the latter 19th Century, industrial development once again flourished in New Jersey. The railroad boom solved its internal transportation problems. International trade had become an important factor. Most important of all, there was a mass migration of shops and factories into New Jersey from the crowded urban metropolitan areas of New York and Philadelphia. This movement was abetted by the state's less hostile tax policies. Although too late to participate more fully in the 19th Century industrial revolution, New Jersey did finally evolve into a major industrial state.

Contributors to the industrial development of America should include Delaware. Small as the state is, it provided an indispensable ingredient. Almost all of the black powder used in the nation for weapons or for mining and construction was manufactured there. It seems that before the Duponts arrived, black powder was manufactured locally. It was unreliable and very dangerous to use. Dupont, by exercising extreme care during the manufacturing process, produced a black powder that was so reliable, that it virtually cornered the American market. Interestingly, today Dupont is more widely known for its nylon than for its explosives.

The industrial development, which took place in New York in the early and mid 19th Century, was so great and so important that its evolution will be covered in a separate chapter. New York led the nation from the mini industrial revolution, which began in New England, into a full-fledged industrial revolution, resulting in the United States becoming the industrial giant of the world.

CHAPTER XVI

INDUSTRIAL DEVELOPMENT

NEW YORK

As outlined in Chapter XIV, there are three legs to the industrial development stool: people (#1), transportation infrastructure (#2), and power (#3). In the early 19th Century, New York began its industrial revolution with leg #2 already in place.

It had its genesis in the magnificent harbor of the Port of New York. It was spacious, deep, wide, with quick and easy access to the ocean. Of equal importance in the 19th Century, it also had direct waterborne access to all points of the compass: north via the Hudson River, east via the Long Island Sound; west and Canada via the Erie Canal; and south via the New Jersey cross-state canals. No other port in the nation could claim such a judicious location with so many physical advantages. Writers in the 19th Century, repeatedly referred to it as the busiest and most exciting port in the world.

The other part of New York's natural transportation infrastructure was the Hudson River. It was so deep and navigable that Henry Hudson thought it would lead him to the Pacific Ocean. Unlike the turbulent waters in New England or the shallow and slow moving rivers of the south and west, the Hudson provided ocean navigability for over 150 miles up to Albany, an early and important seaport for the new nation.

What nature did not provide, the people of New York provided for themselves. They created a magnificent internal canal system, second to none in the nation. It was not restricted to only the Erie Canal. It consisted of a whole network of canals, stretching over 850 miles and covering almost the entire state of New York (see Chapter VII). The network included the Black

River Canal, Oswego Canal, Genesee Valley Canal, Seneca Canal, Crooked Lake Canal, Chenango Canal, plus countless feeders, inlets, and extensions. Most important, for purposes of this book, was the Delaware & Hudson Canal. Although not an official part of the New York State canal system, because it was privately funded and built, it had direct access via the Hudson River to all of the canals and waterways in the state.

The canal system of New York not only fulfilled the requirements for leg #2 of the development stool, but helped create leg #1, "people." As noted in Chapter XIV, the first wave of immigrants consisted mostly of people fleeing persecution, and the second wave were mostly people seeking land and a farm of their own. However, by the mid 19th Century, the nature of the immigrants had changed and they became the third wave. This was the group that provided most of the "people" needed to form leg #1 of the development stool.

New York City was their point of entry into the United States and tens of thousands remained there. Others followed the state's excellent transportation system and flowed into the many cities springing up all over the state. The immigrants tended to congregate in urban areas and form communities of their own. There, they worked in whatever factory was located nearby. The remainder of the immigrants were recruited to work in factories, mines, and mills elsewhere.

The immigrant communities became vibrant, dynamic, and contributed enormously to the culture and economy of the nation. They even became some of the best customers for the products that they and their fellow immigrants were producing. Of course, there were some growing pains. Probably the most notable example was the draft riots in New York City. Because of unfair draft laws during the Civil War, immigrants staged the most violent riots (1000 fatalities) that the nation had witnessed. President Lincoln had to send troops from the Battle of Gettysburg to regain control of the city. Once order was restored, New York continued on its way to become the Empire State of the nation, helped in no small measure by the participants in the riot.

For the state of New York, the "power" leg, #3 of the industrial development stool, presented a problem. Waterpower had its limitations. Had New York chosen that course of action, its industrial development would have reached a plateau and stagnated, much the same as New England. Its only option was the steam engine. There was no other alternative. It is a fact upon which all economists seem to agree: it was the steam engine, which powered all of the major world's industrial revolutions during the 18th and 19th centuries.

As wood became less plentiful and more expensive, coal became the only economical viable substitute which could be used as fuel for the steam engines. However, the coal New York needed for its steam engines was in Pennsylvania. The only cost effective way of transporting it to New York was via the Delaware & Hudson Canal. Ocean shipping was too expensive. Later, using the cross state canals of New Jersey would have delayed New York's industrial revolution by 20-30 years. Also, the coal would have been more expensive (too many middlemen,) causing products manufactured in New York to be less competitive.

The Delaware & Hudson Canal Company provided New York with the millions and millions of tons of coal that it needed and at the cheapest price. Since it owned the mines, the transportation system and the distribution network, no other company could sell its coal in New York for less. Of great importance also was the fact that the D&H terminal in New York was located in Kingston/Rondout, about midway between New York's two industrial areas. This made it possible to ship coal, with equal ease, to the factories in both New York City and Upstate New York.

This ability to meet all of New York's needs for coal continued until the end of the 19th Century when railroads took over that responsibility. However, if New York had waited for the railroads to meet its needs for coal, its industrial revolution would have been delayed, and other states would have been as equally competitive. In such a situation, it is quite probable that Pennsylvania would have become the Empire State of the nation. This is borne out by the fact that during the canal era, New York City's population surpassed and almost doubled that of Philadelphia. However, during the railroad era, the population differential between New York City and Philadelphia remained relatively constant.

Once the state of New York had its three legs (people, transportation, and power) of the industrial development stool firmly in place, it began its industrial revolution in a very intense manner. At the same time, the Delaware & Hudson Canal Company made so many improvements to its canal that it increased its capacity tenfold. New York's industrial revolution made similar advancements. It quickly became the nation's number one industrial state, surpassing the next two states combined. New York's position continued well into the 20th Century, making it the true Empire State of the nation.

In discussing New York's industrial revolution, it should be noted that there are really two New Yorks. One is the metropolitan area of New York City. The other is everything north of Westchester County and west of New England, more popularly referred to as Upstate New York. Industrially, economically, and in terms of population, they are almost co-equal.

First, let us examine briefly the City of New York. The harbor of New York was and is magnificent. It is very close to the ocean and has easy access to water routes north, south, east, and west. So ideal was its location, that during the Revolutionary War, the British captured it and made it the center of all of their military operations in the colonies. After

Courtesy: Hudson River Valley Maritme Museum, Kingston, NY

Delaware & Hudson Coal Distribution Center
Island Dock, Kingston/Rondout, NY

the British evacuated it in 1783, the city began to expand, and for a short three year period, it was the capital of the new nation.

Its population and economic growth began as an indirect result of the introduction of steam boat service on the Hudson River by Robert Fulton in 1807. Once the Erie Canal began operations in 1825, the city's growth was even more rapid, but still not at an exponential rate. That type of growth rate had to wait until after 1828 when the Delaware & Hudson Canal could provide it with an abundant and cheap source of "power." This, coupled with an almost coincidental arrival of the "third wave" of immigrants, caused the growth rate to achieve exponential levels. By the year 1840, there were over 3,000,000 people in the city of New York, making it the largest city in the nation. As an historical footnote, by the year 1830, New York even boasted of a gas lighting system to illuminate its streets. Prior to that time, every 7th house was required to hang a lantern from a second floor window to provide street illumination.

It should be mentioned that at that time, the city had one serious handicap. It lacked an adequate supply of fresh potable water. It had to rely upon thousands of private and public wells. Since the outdoor privy was the common method of human waste disposal, it presented a serious health problem. The solution came in the form of the great Croton Dam and Water System, which began construction in 1835 and was completed in 1843. It included an enormous 41 mile aqueduct system, which supplied over 95,000,000 gallons of clean water to the city each day. Later, it was enlarged with the Ashokan and Delaware Lackawack reservoirs, but the basic system is still in use today. The water of New York City is rated as the best of any major city in the world. Two items of note: the water system was designed and built by John Jervis, builder of the D&H Canal, and it was built with Rosendale cement.

During the 19th Century, the city of New York was converted from just a commercial business and trading center into the largest manufacturing complex in the nation. Its industrial revolution did not rely upon one or two dominant industries, such as iron or textiles, but upon thousands and thousands of small and medium size factories, all located in its metropolitan urban area. These factories produced goods not only for their respective urban areas, but also for all other areas serviced by New York's transportation infrastructure. It is almost impossible to enumerate the variety and quantity of goods manufactured and sold. Records indicate that by the end of the 19th Century, there were over 25,000 shops and factories in the New York metropolitan area. It led the nation in the number of factories, number of factory workers, factory output, and factory investment.

Almost everyone is familiar with the garment industry of New York. It had its origins in the 19th Century. While New England and other areas produced the basic textiles, it was New York which fashioned them into dresses, suits, clothing, hats, and bustles, that the people wore, not only in the nation, but all over the world. They also produced some of the finest laces, embroideries, and other dry goods for the nation. The garment industry occupied almost all of mid-town Manhattan and is still vibrant even into the 21st century.

It was a common practice in the 19th Century for manufacturers of similar items to cluster themselves into specific districts. These industrial districts made good business sense for manufacturing, wholesale, and retail purposes. As with the garment district, some of these districts are still functional today.

One of the earliest manufacturing districts was the "leather district" in lower Manhattan. Hundreds of types of leather products were produced there, from belting and harnesses to purses and billfolds. At that time, leather belting was at a premium. This was the era before composite and web belting, and the most widely used method of transmitting power throughout a factory was by means of leather belting. The factories of the time were inundated with shafts, pulleys, and wheels, all connected with leather belts. This was especially so in textile mills. It may seem odd to mention, but the entire leather district was permeated with the pleasing smell of polished leather. The odor became so popular that in later years, it was even used in aftershave lotions.

Without doubt, the district with the most pleasing aroma was the coffee district, also in lower Manhattan. In this district, coffee was imported, roasted, ground, and packaged for the retail market. The coffee district, and to some extent the surrounding area, blossomed with the delicious aroma of early morning coffee. It was rumored that many passengers rode the rickety Third Avenue El through the district just so that they could sit back and enjoy that fresh coffee aroma.

In New York City there were districts for the manufacture and sale of virtually every consumer oriented product. There was even a district for dolls and stuffed toys. The "district" concept included products made of wood, iron, and steel. There were ship building areas as well as districts for foundries and chemicals. The list of factories and products is endless. As noted earlier, one of the largest steam engine and boiler factories in the nation was in Brooklyn.

One business sector which deserves special mention is the publishing industry. It was important then and is still important today. By 1850, New York was the publishing center of the nation. It was estimated that between 1865 and 1885, there were over 3,000 magazines and periodicals published in the city. Further, it was estimated that by 1899, one half of all of the publishing in the United States took place in New York. Still today, there is an expression, "If you want to have a book published, go to New York." There was one sad incident in the publishing business during the 19th Century. A steam boiler used to power the printing presses on 26th Street exploded, resulting in 67 fatalities. This was the era before electricity, and the only source of power available, excluding the water wheel, was the steam engine.

Besides being the largest manufacturing center in the nation, New York was also the center for all of the ancillary services associated with trade and commerce. By the end of the 19th Century, the amount of cargo passing through the harbor of New York was equal to that of all of the other ports in the nation, combined.

Industrial development in Upstate New York equaled that of New York City in virtually every category, such as people involved, output of goods, monies invested, and economic activity. However, manufacturing in Upstate New York was not limited to one or two districts, but was spread throughout the entire state. If there was any such thing as a concentration of industries, it was probably in the Albany, Schenectady, and Troy triangle.

Albany, as the capital of New York, got its start as a fur trading center long before the Revolutionary War. It was one of the major seaports for the colonies into the 19th Century. During the canal era, it was the terminus of the Erie and Lake Champlain Canals. At that time, it was not unusual to see as many as 1,000 barges, sloops, schooners, ships, barques, and canal boats tied up at its docks, piers, and quays. Not only was it a major trading center, but it was well-known for its wood and paper products, its machinery and metal products, as well as its textiles.

Schenectady became a major manufacturing center as early as 1840, when the American Locomotive factory began its operations. It later became one of the largest manufacturers of steam locomotives in the nation. Schenectady was also widely known for the manufacture of many building products, from insulation materials to paints and varnishes. Its most important manufacturing achievement began in the late 19th Century when Thomas Edison moved a workshop from New Jersey to Schenectady. It was the genesis for the giant General Electric Corporation.

Completing the triangle was Troy. It was a key player in the industrial revolution of New York. During the early 19th Century, it was the iron and steel center of the state. It was famous for its stoves, nails, stagecoaches, and horse drawn carriages. Most noteworthy of all was the fact that the iron and steel plates for the warship *Monitor*, of Civil War fame, were fabricated there. Also noteworthy was the fact that Troy was famous for the invention and manufacture of men's detachable collars and cuffs, very popular at that time. It produced quality textile products and was the home of Samuel Wilson, more popularly known as Uncle Sam. To this day, the phrase "Troy Built," connotes excellence in metal products. The Shaker religious community originated in nearby Watervliet in 1776. They were renown nationwide for the excellence of their furniture and other products. Many an old timer can still remember when "Shaker Salt" was the premier and most sought after salt on the market.

On the Hudson River, there was West Point. Today, it is known as the home of the US Military Academy. However, in 1838, West Point was more widely known for its foundry, which was one of the largest manufacturers of large (20+ HP) steam engines in the nation. Across the river, was Poughkeepsie. By the latter part of the 19th Century, it was well-known for its beer, Smith Brothers cough drops, and office machines. One beer owner was so successful that he later founded Vassar College for women. Nearby Newburgh, besides being a headquarters for George Washington during the Revolution, was a large producer of men's clothing and women's apparel.

Initially, Syracuse was renown for its nearby salt deposits. By mid 19th Century, these salt deposits accounted for about 60% of all salt used in the United States. One of the earliest plans for the Erie Canal was that it would extend only as far as Syracuse. Later Syracuse became a center for machine tools and all types of metal products. Nearby Rome became the home of, and excelled in, the manufacture of almost any product made of copper or brass.

Two cities which deserve mention are Corning and Oneida. Corning began as a utopian community in 1835. Today, it is world famous for its glass products, not only for Corning Ware, but also for Steuben Glass. In 1848, Oneida also began as a utopian/religious community. The city became famous for its quality tableware and silver products. In 1881, Oneida had to change from a religious community to a private corporation due to public pressure. Polygamy was the problem. The members believed that everyone was married to everyone else.

Buffalo, now the second largest city in the state, was merely a trading post until the completion of the Erie Canal. It grew into the state's most important city on the Great Lakes, with its population quadrupling in the first seven years. It was a city through which hundreds of thousands of immigrants and millions of tons of grain flowed. The world's first steam powered grain elevator was built there. By the late 19th Century, Buffalo literally exploded in size and activity. Today, it can produce almost any desired product as long as it is made of metal.

Originally, Rochester grew as a short cut, via the Genesee River, to Lake Ontario. The Erie Canal flowed right through the center of the city. At first, it was renown for its very large grain milling capacity, which serviced the thriving grain farmers of western New York. Then it became a major builder of canal boats, over 200 per year. By mid 19th Century, it became a center for eyeglass manufacturing. After Bausch & Lomb was established, it became the optics center for the nation. Shortly thereafter, another mammoth industry had its origins in Rochester. Kodak became the world's largest supplier of film and photographic equipment. Another footnote in history: the Mormon religion had its origins there.

Not to be forgotten is the three-city area of Endicott, Binghamton, and Johnson City. By the end of the 19th Century, the Endicott-Johnson shoe was considered to be the premier shoe of the nation. Office machines and equipment were also manufactured there. In 1918, one of these small companies changed its name to International Business Machines (IBM).

The list of manufacturing accomplishments in Upstate New York during the 19th Century is almost endless. Even small cities participated in the industrial revolution. Two typical examples are Gloversville and Tannersville. Both became famous nationwide and were so named for the quantity and quality of their respective products.

The preceding examples were cited to give the reader some understanding of the enormity of the industrial revolution, which made New York the Empire State of the nation. Before the 19th Century, New York was agriculturally oriented and ranked only seventh in population. By the end of the 19th Century, New York was number one in both population and in industrial production. This could not have taken place without an abundant, reliable and cheap source of power, the third leg of the development stool. It was the millions of tons of coal carried over the Delaware & Hudson Canal that provided the fuel for the steam engines, which in turn powered New York's unbelievable industrial revolution. Put succinctly: no Rosendale cement, no D&H Canal, no coal, no industrial revolution.

CHAPTER XVII

ALTERNATIVE SUPPLIERS OF COAL

It has been suggested that New York could have had and did have suppliers of coal other than the D&H Canal Company. This was true, but without D&H coal, New York could not have achieved its unbelievable industrial revolution. This chapter will examine the other options.

It must be remembered that there were only three major deposits of anthracite coal in the United States. All were in eastern Pennsylvania; more popularly known as Schuylkill (south), Lehigh (central), and Lackawanna (north), which included D&H coal. Coal was shipped to New York from each of these deposits. The enormous deposits of bituminous coal were not factored into the equation because they were located in the Western regions of the Appalachian Mountains and not easily accessible to the eastern markets. They had to wait for the railroad era (the second leg of the industrial development stool) before soft coal became the optimal source of energy for industry.

After the Revolutionary War, New York ranked number 7 in population. It was an agriculturally oriented state and was often referred to as the breadbasket of the nation. Without D&H coal, New York could not have risen during the 19th Century from its humble agricultural beginnings to become the most industrially dominant state in the nation. The reasons for this are many and involve such factors as geographic location, logistical thru-put capacity, product/marketing costs, and windows of opportunity.

This chapter will apply these factors to the four alternative suppliers of coal to New York and show clearly that either singly or combined, they could not have replaced the coal carried by the D&H Canal. The four alternative suppliers of coal were as follows:

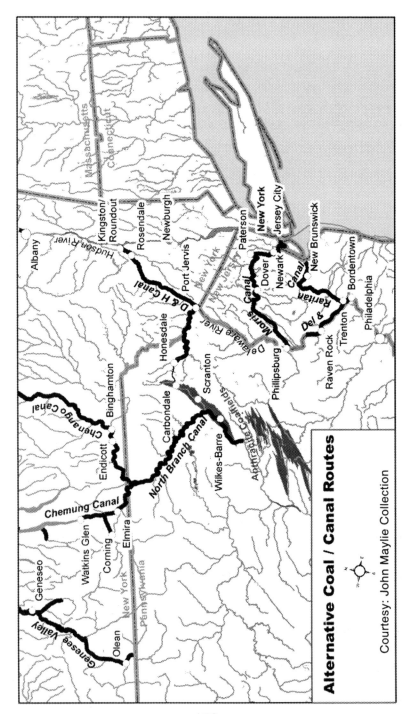

Alternative Coal / Canal Routes

Courtesy: John Maylie Collection

(1) Sailing Ships
(2) Delaware & Raritan Canal (Trenton to New Brunswick)
(3) Morris Canal (Phillipsburg to Jersey City)
(4) Chenango/Chemung/Junction/North Branch Canal System

Philadelphia was the main coal distribution center for the sailing ships. They supplied coal to New England, seaports along the Atlantic coast, and foreign ports as well. The coal came to Philadelphia from the southern (Schuylkill) and central (Lehigh) deposits via several local canals. There the barges were unloaded, and the coal was heaped in huge stockpiles along the Delaware River. Sailing ships were then loaded with coal from these stockpiles. At their destination, the coal was then unloaded onto similar stockpiles. Finally, the coal was sold and moved to the end users.

This was the era before the advent of bulk handling machinery. It was a man with a shovel that moved the coal at these transfer points. In most instances, ownership of the coal also changed at each transfer point. This multiple handling of coal and the multiple transfer of ownership increased the price of coal for the end user. Thus, products manufactured using this coal were no longer competitive in the market place, and industrial development in such areas stagnated.

It will be left to historians, with their numerous research assistants and statisticians, to calculate the number of sailing ships available, the tonnage they could carry, the cost of coal at each transfer point, etc. However, for purposes of this book the obvious example of New England's fall from industrial supremacy will serve to demonstrate the point beyond dispute.

By the time the D&H Canal became operational in 1828, New England was well into its mini industrial revolution. It was powered by the waterwheel. As the industrial revolution continued to grow, available waterpower reached its limit. New England began to use the steam engine fueled with coal to supplement the abundant supply of waterpower. Sailing ships were used to provide the coal. However, sailing ships could not even meet these modest demands. New England's industrial expansion halted and later began to decline. It therefore follows that if sailing ships could not meet New England's modest needs for coal, sailing ships would be unable to satisfy New York's insatiable appetite for coal to meet the needs of its industrial revolution.

Finally, it should be mentioned that if New York relied on coal shipped on sailing ships, only metropolitan New York City would have been the beneficiary. Upstate New York, which accounted for one-half of New York's industrial production, would have been starved for fuel to meet its industrial needs, and its industrialization would never have taken place.

The next alternative supplier of coal to New York was the Delaware & Raritan Canal. It appeared to be the most likely choice. The Canal was only 44 miles long, and it was the most direct route from the coalfields of Pennsylvania to New York City. It had no serious geographic obstacles to overcome, and water supply for the canal was not a problem. There are indications that William Pitt recommended such a canal over 100 years earlier. Also, the need for such a canal was included in the Gallatin Report of 1808, which outlined the inland transportation requirements of the nation. The canal went from Trenton on the Delaware River to the Raritan River near New Brunswick. Once it became fully operational, it was a financial success.

The original charter for the canal gave it a monopoly for cargo and passenger travel between Philadelphia and New York, the two largest cities in the nation. After Chief Justice Roger B. Taney ruled that such a monopoly was illegal, the canal managers made serious attempts to capture the lucrative coal traffic to New York. They built a 21 mile extension to the north from Trenton to Raven Rock to tie into the Lehigh coal deposits. Also, they built an extension southward from Trenton to Bordentown in order to tie into the Schuylkill coal deposits. These extensions paralleled the Delaware River on the Jersey side. They were needed because fully loaded barges, with their tow animals aboard, could not navigate the swift flowing and sometimes turbulent Delaware River. Barges could cross the river safely, as George Washington did during the Revolutionary War, but north-south travel was not an option. Canal barges required a slack water environment and the Delaware River was anything but slack.

In addition to the above, there were a number of outside factors that entered into the situation, which made it impossible for the Delaware & Raritan Canal to fulfill the role of the D&H Canal. First, the Delaware & Raritan Canal provided an indispensable link in the nation's north/south inland waterway system and those users demanded priority in its use. Second, the canal was inundated with passenger and cargo traffic between New York and Philadelphia. This further taxed the thru-put capacity of the canal.

Next, New Brunswick was still about 40-50 miles from the New York industrial areas. New York was still claiming jurisdiction over the Hudson River, thereby creating an impediment for New Jersey barge travel. Waterways, which were under control of the State of New Jersey, flowed through the Jersey industrial areas and population centers. As a result, almost all of the coal shipped via the Delaware & Raritan Canal was destined for New Jersey customers. Finally, despite the fact that the Delaware & Raritan Canal could tap the resources of both the Lehigh and Schuylkill coal deposits, even during its peak years, the amount of coal it carried never exceeded 1/3 of that carried by the D&H Canal.

Another factor which should be mentioned is that the Delaware & Raritan Canal missed the optimum period for its window of opportunity. It was not completed until 8 years after the

D&H Canal and not fully operational until a few years later. This extended into the beginning of the railroad era, which further detracted from its operational capabilities.

Finally, because of the geographic location of the Delaware & Raritan Canal, the coal it carried would have benefited only the New York City industrial areas. Upstate New York would have been starved for fuel, thereby negating its industrial development. In contrast, the D&H Canal terminated at almost the exact juncture of the two co-equal New York's, Upstate New York and New York City. It could service both areas with equal ease and efficiency.

Another alternative supplier of coal for New York was the 102 mile Morris Canal. It ran across northern New Jersey, from Phillipsburg on the Delaware River to Jersey City on the Hudson River. At the time, it was considered an engineering marvel. In addition to water supply problems, it had to overcome a rise and fall in elevation of 1674 feet. This was accomplished by a system of 24 locks and 23 inclined planes over which barges on cradles were moved. Since there was a limit as to how much a cradle could carry, the barges were built in sections. The barges had to be disassembled and the sections loaded on cradles separately. Then, each section had to be hauled over the inclined planes individually and re-joined on the far side, much like those on Pennsylvania's Main Line Canal.

Initially, the canal was so mismanaged and burdened with fraud and embezzlement that the managers had to spend most of their time avoiding criminal prosecution. By 1841, the canal company collapsed. Later it was reorganized under new management and operated successfully well into the 20th Century. One of the reasons that the canal was successful was that it had a "lock" on the northern New Jersey market. The industrial centers of Passaic, Patterson, Newark, and Jersey City were along its route.

Coal was the principal cargo carried on the Morris Canal. At first, the canal company tried to compete with the D&H Canal for the New York City market. They found that even when combined with the Lehigh coal companies in Pennsylvania, they could not do so. This was despite the fact that D&H Canal coal had to travel 100 miles further. They could not compete in terms of price or quantity. As for price, they simply could not match the superior management and efficiency of the D&H Canal Company. Due to the vertical nature of the D&H Canal Company, it controlled every aspect of coal supply from the mine from which the coal was extracted to the coal bins of the end users. Coal supplied by the Morris Canal was not that fortunate. There were too many middlemen, each requiring a profit, resulting in their coal being at a price disadvantage.

Because of the route and the design of the Morris canal, there was a finite limit as to how much coal it could carry. Even during its most prolific periods, it never carried more than 1/5th of the coal carried by the D&H Canal. As with the Delaware & Raritan Canal, there was no excess capacity that could be diverted to satisfy the enormous requirements of the New York market.

Another negating factor for the Morris Canal was its geographic location. Similar to the Delaware & Raritan Canal, it was oriented completely to the New York City market. It could not service the Upstate New York market, which constituted one half of New York's industrial production.

The final alternative supplier of coal for the New York market was the North Branch/Junction/Chenango/Chemung Canal System in northern Pennsylvania and western New York. Its purpose was to carry coal from the Lackawanna coal deposits in northern Pennsylvania, up along the Susquehanna River, to the Elmira/Binghamton industrial areas of New York, and on to the great Erie Canal market place.

The North Branch Canal System possessed a number of inherent problems, which could not be overcome. As a result, it became the most expensive canal failure in Pennsylvania's history.

The management of the system was divided between two different states, not always in amicable relations with each other. Also, there were at least five different canal companies involved in the management of the system. This alone created so many middlemen and fingers in the pie that the coal could not be sold to customers at a competitive price. Some coal was sold in the Elmira and Binghamton market areas, but they failed to penetrate the great Erie Canal market.

The location of the North Branch Canal System in western New York made it impossible to service both the New York City market and the Upstate New York Market. When compared to the amount of coal carried by the D&H Canal, the amount of coal carried by the North Branch Canal System was negligible (about 1%).

To further contribute to failure of the system , its construction was not completed until 1858, thereby completely missing its window of opportunity. The railroad era was approaching its peak, and the railroads could service the smaller, widespread markets of western New York much better than the large expensive North Branch Canal System.

The question of timeliness, or window of opportunity, was mentioned several times and may need further explanation. The height of the canal building frenzy and canal transportation dominance was from 1820 until 1860 when over 4,000 miles of canals were built in the United States. Although, the first small railroad trunk lines began operating as early as 1831, it could be said that the railroad era officially began in 1853 when the New York Central railroad company was firmly established. That was when it finished consolidating all of the small railroads along the Erie Canal into one large railroad company, stretching 365 miles, all the way from Albany to

Buffalo. New canal construction ceased a few years later. This meant that the D&H Canal, having seized its window of opportunity, had a jump start on all of the three alternative canals, which had not been completed until 8 to 28 years later. By the time the alternative canals went through their growing pains and began to operate efficiently, they were already beginning to feel the warm breath of railroad competition.

The D&H Canal Company realized the importance of the railroads, and around 1860, they began to acquire them. By the end of the 19th Century, it had become one of the largest railroad companies in the nation. The D&H Company had over 900 miles of track in the states of New York and Pennsylvania and was able to service its customers with equal ease and efficiency. As a matter of record, it was so capable and efficient that it became the target of the federal government. Because of the vertical nature of the company and its ownership of the railroads, it was subjected to years of litigation under the guise of the Anti-trust Act. The government wanted to dismember the company. It was very similar to the government actions later against Rockefeller's Standard Oil Company and the Bill Gates Microsoft Company of modern times.

In view of the above, it can be stated as an irrefutable fact, that none of the four alternative suppliers of coal, either singly or in combination, could have provided the entire state New York with the enormous quantity of coal needed for its unprecedented industrial revolution during the 19th Century. Without the coal to fuel its industrial revolution, New York's industrial development would have stagnated, and New England might have continued its industrial dominance. It is also quite possible that the Philadelphia/Delaware Bay area might have become the nation's industrial center. However, the coal from the D&H Canal resulted in New York becoming the Empire State, in fact, as well as in name.

CHAPTER XVIII

THANK ROSENDALE

It all began with the discovery of "gray gold" in Rosendale. This enormous deposit of nature's own perfect mix of lime, silica, and alumina produced the natural cement, which became the foundation upon which New York's 19th Century economy was built.

Rosendale cement not only provided for the physical construction of New York's industrial base, but also was a key factor in the financing, building, and successful operation of the Delaware & Hudson Canal. It was the D&H Canal Company that provided New York with the millions upon millions of tons of coal that it needed to power its unparalleled industrial growth.

A mini-industrial revolution had already begun in New England. However, it was powered by the water wheel, and soon reached its limit, beyond which it could expand no further.

In the meantime, two additional factors appeared on the scene, which contributed to New York's industrial development. The first was Robert Fulton's steamboat. It modernized New York's natural transportation infrastructure and made possible the unexcelled flow of people, trade, and commerce in and throughout the state. The second was Oliver Evans' "non-condensing" steam engine. It was relatively compact, easily moved, and ideally suited to power New York's industrial revolution.

By mid 19th Century, New York had in place the three mandatory legs of the industrial development stool, people, transportation infrastructure, and power. They were possessed to such an overwhelming degree, that New York leap-frogged all other states and became the industrial leader of the nation.

On the cover of this book is a reproduction of a sketch by Currier & Ives of New York's spacious and bustling harbor, including the Brooklyn Bridge. Reconstruction of the sketch indicates that it depicted the harbor as seen from the Torch being held in the hand of the newly erected Statue of Liberty. It must have been the image that was created in the mind of Auguste Bartholdi its sculptor, a few years earlier.

The Statue of Liberty had an interesting beginning. The movement was started around 1865 by Professor Edouard-Rene Lefebvre de Laboulaye of the College de France in Paris. He wanted to celebrate 100 years of American independence and to honor President Lincoln for freeing the slaves. Frederic Auguste Bartholdi, the sculptor, traveled to the United States in 1871 to help organize an acceptance committee, which would be responsible for all related details in this country. He traveled throughout the nation and met with the President, members of Congress, the poet Longfellow, and hundreds of other leaders who might be interested in the project. It is rumored that Senator Sumner of Massachusetts tried to propose a site in Boston.

The high point of the visit for the sculptor Bartholdi was when his ship docked in New York. He was totally astonished and amazed at what he saw. New York's magnificent harbor was a veritable forest of ships' masts, as far as the eye could see. No other harbor in the world could equal it. At that time, New York was at the very pinnacle of its industrial revolution. Bartholdi could hardly believe the vitality, the energy, and the commercial activity that was taking place. The vibrancy, the enthusiasm, and the positive outlook on life itself were beyond that of anything he had seen on earth. It was at that moment that he vowed to do all in his power to insure that his edifice would be erected in the harbor of New York.

Professor Lefebure de Laboulaye, the leader of the project, had assumed naturally that the statue would be located in the nation's capital, as was customary in Europe. Bartholdi, on his return to France, spent almost five years trying to convince Professor Edouard-Rene LeFebvre that the statue should be in New York. He finally succeeded, and the rest is history. There was no other logical reason for selecting New York other than the fact that it was in the midst of an industrial revolution, exceeding that of any other city, or country on earth.

The twin towers of the World Trade Center, another New York City icon, had its origins because of the dire need for the city to erect more office space to meet its requirements. The principal motivating factor was the industrial revolution, which began in the 19th Century and continued to grow into the 20th Century. However, for New York City, its character changed, and the city drifted into a haven for business, finance, and corporate management. There was an ever increasing demand for quality office space, as opposed to the factory and warehouse space requirements of the 19th Century. Manhattan, being an island and fortunately located on a bed rock of solid stone, had no alternative but to expand vertically.

Having the World Trade Center at its chosen location had the additional advantage of ridding the city of one of the few remaining blighted areas in lower Manhattan. It was simply not fitting for the world's financial center to be adjacent to a grimy area of piers, docks, and warehouses of a bygone age. The dinginess of the area can be verified by the author. He once labored there as a baggage handler for the New York Central Railroad at the Wheehawken/Courtlandt Street Ferry Station.

The World Trade Center complex was so large and important that it took the joint efforts of both New York and New Jersey to implement it. Under the mantle of the New York and New Jersey Port Authority, it was conceived, constructed, managed, and operated. It lived up to expectations and had as many as 10,000 persons working in the complex. If New

York had not been the Empire State of the nation, there would have been no need for such a grandiose edifice. If one was eventually required, it probably would have been built in Philadelphia.

In summary, all that has happened in New York, until the modern era, was the direct or indirect result of New York's industrial revolution that took place during the 19th Century. It was an industrial revolution which could not have taken place without a reliable, abundant, cheap source of power. That power came from the tens of thousands of steam engines fueled by the millions of tons of coal brought to New York via the Delaware & Hudson Canal. At that time, there was no viable substitute for this coal. No other coal could have been brought to New York in such quantities and distributed at such a competitive price, except by means of the Delaware & Hudson Canal.

In view of the above, it then follows (as surely as night follows day,) that the discovery of Rosendale cement initiated a chain of events, which resulted in the building of the Delaware & Hudson Canal, which, in turn provided the fuel for New York's 19th Century industrial revolution, making it the Empire State of the nation. Therefore, for whatever New York is today, whether positive or negative, one can say without hesitation, THANK ROSENDALE.

REFLECTIONS

While doing the research for this book, especially as concerns monuments of progress, the author recalled to mind comments he had heard on July 4th, 1971. The comments were made by The Most Reverend Bishop Fulton J. Sheen on the steps of the Lincoln Memorial during the ceremonies of Honor America Day. He suggested that a giant monolith be erected at the entrance to San Francisco's harbor, with the word RESPONSIBILITY emblazoned across the top. Then, he mused, the whole world would understand that the United States embraces not only freedom, but "Freedom with Responsibility."

ACKNOWLEDGMENTS

First and foremost, I would like to acknowledge the invaluable assistance of my sister, Rita Pfeifer, my advisor, mentor, editor and walking encyclopedia of early Rosendale.

During the review process, I was helped immeasurably by Larry Lowenthal, author of, *From the Coalfields to the Hudson,* Peter Genero Jr., Ulster County Railroad and Canal enthusiast, Jeanne Bollendorf, Executive Director, D&H Canal Historical Society, and Ann Gilchrist, Rosendale Town Historian.

Of singular importance was the innovative work of John Maylie, cartographer, for the excellent maps used in this book.

Next, I would like to thank Judy Jenkins and Grace Bianculli, proof-readers, Florence Prusmack, President of the Fort Pierce Writer's Club, and all of the members for their reviews, comments, and guidance. Also included is Gordon Verro and the staff at Wizard of Ink Printing, for their technical advice and assistance.

Finally, there were a number of oral historians, who provided many of the sidelights included in this book, but who, unfortunately are no longer with us:

Beatovic, Mary and Ivo
Ellsworth, Andy
Genero, Anthony
Huben, Steve
Kern, Leo
Kopp, Ray
Madden, Katie
Miani, Fred and Lillian
Miani, Mary and Joseph
Rosa, Kenny
Vaughn, Doc

Technical support and illustrations were provided by:

Century House Historical Society
D&H Canal Historical Society
Henry Ford Museum
Hudson River Maritime Museum
Kingston Senate House Historic Site
Minisink Valley Historical Society
New York State Canal Corporation
New York State Division of Tourism
New York State Department of Transportation
New York State Thruway Authority
The J. Maylie Collection
The Ted Hazen Collection
US Merchant Marine Academy Museum

Technological assistance was provided by cement and commodity specialist and mineral & material analysts of the US Coast and Geodetic Service. They also provided:

Contour Maps
Country Quadrangle Maps
Highway Maps
Image Maps
Relief Maps
Topographic Maps
US Base Maps

Other Maps:

Distribution of Pennsylvania Coal, Map 11,
    Commonwealth of Pennsylvania
Department of Conservation and Natural Resources,
    Bureau of Topographic and Geologic Survey, 1992
D&R Canal State Park Map, New Jersey State Park Service, 2002
Eastern US Wall Map, American Map Corporation, 1995
Profile Map of Morris Canal, Rand McNally, 1921
Railway Map of the State of Pennsylvania, J.A. Caldwell, 1877
Road Atlas, Rand McNally, 1999

BIBLIOGRAPHY

Bourne, Russell. *Floating West* Norton Press, 1992

Cotton, Julia M. *Annals of Old Manhattan.* Brentano's, 1901

Earle, Alice Morse. *Colonial Days of Old New York.* Charles Scribner's and Sons, 1896

Edmonds, Walter D. *Rome Haul.* Little Brown & Co., 1929

Ernest, R. & Dupuy, Trevor, N. *The Harper Encyclopedia of Military History, Fourth Edition.* Harper Collins Publishers, 1993

Evers, Alf. *The Catskills.* Doubleday & Company, 1972

Depew, Chauncey M. *United States Industrial Revolution of the 19th Century.* Hubert H. Bancroft, 1901

Gilchrist, Ann. *Footsteps Across Cement.* Self Published, 1997

Granick, Harry. *Underneath New York.* Fordham University Press, 1947

Haris, Jonathan. *The Statue for America.* Four Winds Press, 1985

Hislop, Codman. *The Mohawk River.* Rinehart & Co., 1948

Hunter, Louis C. *History of Industrial Power in the United States 1870-1930, Volume I.* University Press of Virginia, 1979

Hunter, Louis C. *History of Industrial Power in the United States 1870-1930, Volume II.* University Press of Virginia, 1985

Keller, Allan. *Life Along the Hudson.* Sleep Hollow Press, 1976

Knickerbocker, Dedrich (Washington Irving).
A History of New York. The Heritage Press, 1940

L'Amour, Louis. *How the West Was Won.* LGT L'Amour, 1988

LeRoy, Edwin D. *The Delaware and Hudson Canal.*
Wayne County Historical Society, 1950

Licht, Walter. *Industrializing America.* John Hopkins Press, 1995

Long, Priscilla. *Where the Sun Never Shines.* Paragon Press, 1987

Lowenthal, Larry. *From Coal Fields to the Hudson.* Purple Mountain Press, 1997

Mabee, Carlton. *Listen to the Whistle.* Purple Mountain Press, 1995

Morrison, Samuel Elliott. *Erie Canal.* Harvard University Press, 1901

Neal, Harry Edward. *From Spinning Wheel to Space Craft.* Julia Messner Inc., 1964

Routledge, Robert. *Discoveries and Inventions of the Nineteenth Century.*
Crescent Books, 1989

Sale, Kirkpatrick. *The Fire of His Genius.* The Free Press, 2001

Shaw, Robert E. *Canals for a Nation.* University Press of Kentucky, 1992

Shaw, Robert E. *Erie Water West.* University Press of Kentucky, 1996

Sheriff, Carol. *The Artificial River.* Hill and Wang, 1996

Spangenburg, Ray and Moser, Diane. *Facts on File.* Fort Pierce Public Library, 1992

Truth, Sojourner. *Narrative of Sojourner Truth.* Dictated to Olive Gilbert, 1850

Wakefield, Manville. *Canal Boats to Tidewater.* Steingart Associates Inc., 1992

Weisberger, Bernard A. *Statue of Liberty.* American Heritage, 1985

Witford, Nobel E. *History of Canal Systems of the State of New York, Volume I.* 1905

ENCYCLOPEDIAS:

Academic American Encyclopedia. Grolier Inc., 1998

Colliers Encyclopedia. P. F. Collier, 1997

Encyclopedia Americana. Grolier Inc., 1998

The New Encyclopedia Britanica. Encyclopedia Britanica Inc., 2002

The New Encyclopedia Britanica, Macropaedia. Encyclopedia Britancia Inc., 2002

World Book. World Book Inc., 2002

WEB SITES:

Blasting Rocks, Building Locks and Hauling Coal
http://gsa.confex.com/gsa/2002ne/finalprogram/abstract_30860.htm. (10/26/2002)

Capital and Labor - Invention of the Steam Engine: Roebuck,
http://www.history.rochester.edu/steam/lord/4-2.htm. (3/14/2002)

Capital District, New York State,
http://www.rpi.edu/regional/what_troy.html. (3/27/2003)

Delaware and Hudson Canal,
http://hhr.highlands.com/delaware.html. (10/15/2002)

Delaware and Hudson Canal,
http://www.usgennet.org/usa/ny/county/orange/canal/. (10/25/2002)

Development and Administration of New York State's Canal System,
http://www.archives.nysed.gov/a/researchroom/rr_trans_recrds_dev.shtml. (1/30/2004)

D&H History,
http://www.bridge-line.org/blhs/history.html. (10/26/2002)

Hugh White's Rosendale Cement, http://www.centuryhouse.org/newsletr/win2001/.html. (10/26/2002)

Kingston,
http://www.cr.nps.gov/nr/travel/kingston/transport.htm. (10/25/2002)

Minisink Valley Historical Society,
http://www.minisink.org/delheed.html. (10/25/2002)

Oliver Evans-A revision,
http://www.uh.edu/engines/epi264.htm. (2/24/2004)

Rosendale Big Fire of Sun., Aug 26,1895,
http://widowjane.org/chhs/bigfire/htm. (4/14/2000)

Rotary Steam Engine,
http://www.spartacus.schoolnet.co.uk/texrotary.htm. (5/20/2004)

The Century House Historical Society, History,
http://www.centuryhouse.org/history.html. (10/26/2002)

The CrabtreePhotographs,
http://www.centuryhouse.org/crabtree.html. (1/16/2003)

The Delaware and Hudson Canal, http://www.history.rochester.edu/canal/bib/
whitford/old1906,chapter20,htm. (2/3/2004)

The Delaware and Hudson Canal Company,
http://www.trainweb.org/pt/dh/.html. (10/25/2002)

The Development of the Steam Engine for Pumping,
http://www.rhosybolbock.freeserve.co.uk/steampower-2.htm. (5/4/2004)

The Invention of the Steam Engine,
http://www.his.com/-pshapiro/steam.engine.html. (3/14/2003)

The Library of Congress,
http://www.loc.gov/. (3/27/2003)

The Newcomen Steam Engine,
http://www.technology.niagarae.on.ca/people/mcsele/necomen.htm. (4/20/2004)

Thomas Savery,
http://library.thinkquest.org/coo6011/english/jsites/steam_thomas_savery.php3?v=2.(3/14/2003)

United States Patents the Steamboat,
http://www.history.rochester.edu/steam/dickenson/chapter10.html. (3/15/2003)

Williams Lake,
http://www.willylake.com/html/story03.htm. (10/26/2002)

Work begins on the D&H Canal 1825,
http://www.ci.kingston.ny.us/history/canal.html. (1/25/2002)

Youngfolk's Book of Invention,
http://usgennet.org/usa/topic/preservation/science/inventions/chapter6.htm.(5/4/2004)

Index

A

Albany 8, 14, 15, 21, 27, 57, 58, 59, 66, 80, 96, 111, 113, 114, 143, 150, 162
Alexandria 56, 131
Algonquin Indians 14, 23
Anti-rent Riots 26, 89
Appalachian Mountains 9, 45, 46, 55, 57, 139, 155
Arkwright, Richard 109
Arminia 113
Aspdin, Joseph 31
Austrians 86, 88, 90, 91

B

Baltimore 126, 131
Bartholdi, Frederic Auguste 165, 166
Baxter engine 122
Binghamton 153, 161, 162
Black River Canal 143
Boilers, steam 122, 123, 138, 150
Bolton, John 75, 78
Bordentown 159
Boston 4, 79, 101, 103, 131, 135, 137, 165
Bridgewater Canal 50
British Guiana 17
Bronx 25
Brooklyn 121, 150, 165
Brooklyn Bridge 3, 11, 39, 75, 93, 165
Bruce, Nathaniel 29, 84
Buffalo 57, 58, 59, 60, 66, 152, 163

C

Calhoun, John C. 56
Canals, general (Principal canals indexed separately)
    11, 32, 33, 37, 46, 48, 49, 50, 51, 52, 53, 54, 55, 56, 57, 58, 59, 60, 61,
    62, 63, 130, 131, 133, 134, 137, 139, 140, 144, 145, 146, 151, 156,
    157, 158, 159, 160, 161, 162, 163
Canal du Midi 50
Canarse Indians 14
Carbondale 74, 81
Catholic Church 89, 90
Catskill Mountains 5, 7, 14, 18, 19, 20, 25, 26

Cement 4, 10, 11, 12, 26, 29, 30-41, 70, 71, 77, 78, 82, 84, 85, 86, 87, 88,
    89, 90, 93, 95, 96, 98, 125, 135, 148, 154, 164, 167
Century Cement Company 11, 26, 35, 93
Charcoal 44, 47
Charleston 131, 138
Chenango Canal 144, 156, 157, 161
Chesapeake & Ohio Canal 131
Chicago 62, 132
China 13, 43, 49
Civil War 4, 59, 63, 124, 140, 144, 151
Clermont 109, 110, 111, 112, 113, 114, 116, 119
Clinker 29, 32, 35, 36, 39, 77, 87
Clinton, DeWitt 57
Clinton, George 8
Clinton, Henry 8
Coal 4, 29, 33, 34, 35, 36, 41, 42-48, 60, 62, 64-71, 74-83, 87, 94, 96, 102,
    103, 104, 105, 109, 115, 116, 119, 120, 122, 123, 126, 133, 134, 135,
    138, 139, 140, 145, 146, 147, 154, 155-163, 164, 167
Coke 44, 45
Connecticut 14, 20, 62, 100, 101, 137
Cooperage 37, 38, 77
Corliss, George 121
Corning 152
Corporate management 102, 166
Cotton 28, 98, 100, 135
Crooked Lake Canal 144
Croton Dam 39, 74, 125, 148
Currier & Ives 3, 28, 165

D

Damascus 130
Delaware & Hudson (D&H) Canal 4, 11, 36, 37, 41, 48, 54, 63, 64-73, 74-
    83, 85, 86, 88, 93, 94, 95, 102, 103, 104, 115, 121, 125, 126, 138, 144,
    145, 146, 147, 148, 154, 155, 156, 157, 159, 160, 161, 162, 163, 164, 167
Delaware & Hudson (D&H) Canal Museum 11
Delaware & Hudson Company 82, 83
Delaware River 37, 46, 60, 62, 65, 66, 67, 77, 116, 140, 148, 157, 158,
    159, 160, 163
Delaware State   14, 60, 62, 139, 142
Dickson, Thomas 81
Draft Riots 144

Dupont 142
Durham canal boats 53, 74
Dutch East India Company 13
Dutch Reformed Church 18, 89
Dutch West Indies Trading Company 13, 16

E

Eddyville 7
El Paso 132
Elmira 161, 162
Embargo Act 100
Empire State 3, 63, 94, 125, 145, 146, 153, 163, 166, 167
Endicott 153
Erie Canal 3, 4, 32, 33, 37, 51, 52, 54, 56, 57, 58, 59, 60, 66, 67, 68, 70, 80,
    86, 87, 98, 114, 115, 137, 143, 147, 151, 152, 153, 161, 162
Esopus 9
Evans, Oliver 116, 117, 118, 119, 120, 164

F

Fish 8, 14, 16, 24, 27, 64, 102, 135, 136
Fitch, John 110
Fort Nassau 14
Fort Orange 14
French and Indian War 16, 20, 21, 22, 23, 58
Fulton, Robert 109, 110, 111, 112, 113, 116, 117, 120, 147, 164

G

Gallatin, Albert 56, 156
Genesee Valley Canal 144, 153
Gloversville 153
Grate, Four Dollar 47
Gravity Railroad 67, 74, 75, 81
Gray Gold 3, 11, 34, 41, 70, 71, 85, 91, 164
Grist Mill 7, 20, 25, 26, 36, 97, 98

H

Hamilton, Alexander 55, 56, 136, 141
Hardenbergh, Johannis 19, 21
Hawley 81
Hemlock Bark 26
Hidden Valley 5
High Falls 7, 11, 28, 33, 70, 71, 82, 84, 85, 86
Hone, Philip 68, 75, 76, 77
Honesdale 74, 75, 79

Hudson, Henry 12, 13, 143
Hudson River 5, 7, 8, 13, 14, 15, 19, 20, 23, 25, 27, 51, 57, 59, 60, 66, 67,
    68, 69, 70, 74, 79, 80, 82, 86, 87, 88, 95, 111, 113, 114, 115, 119, 120,
    137, 140, 141, 143, 144, 147, 152, 159, 160
Huguenots 20, 25, 89, 128
Hurley 8, 84

I

Ice Industry 27
Illinois 55, 62
Indiana 55, 62
Industrial development 3, 4, 30, 39, 41, 42, 48, 51, 55, 60, 63, 64, 69, 83,
    94, 95, 96, 101, 102, 103, 104, 105, 113, 115, 116, 117, 121, 122, 123,
    124, 125, 126, 127-134, 135-142, 143-154, 155, 157, 158, 160, 161,
    163, 164-167
Interstate Highway 52, 67, 69
Irish 86, 88, 89, 90, 91, 133, 137,144
Iroquois Indians 14, 23, 25, 58
Irving, Washington 13

J

Jefferson, Thomas 28, 55, 85
Jersey City 129, 157, 160
Jervis, John 68, 74, 75, 125, 148
Johnson City 153
Jones Creek 66
Joppenberg Mountain 91, 92

K

Kansas City 132
Kayak 7
Kidd, Captain 17, 18
Kieft, Willem 16
Kiln, rotary 39, 40, 93
Kilns, vertical 11, 34, 35, 77, 88
Kingston 5, 7, 8, 17, 21, 25,67, 70, 74, 76, 79, 85, 88, 145, 147

L

Lackawanna 65, 68, 155, 161
Lackawaxen River 66, 67
Lake Champlain 8, 58, 80, 87, 151
Lake Erie 51, 57, 58, 59, 62, 66
Lake Ontario 58, 153
LaSalle 45

Lawrenceville 7, 11, 40, 85, 89
Lefebvre, Edouard-Rene de Laboulaye 165, 166
LeFever Falls 7, 78, 85
Lehigh 60, 65, 66, 68, 76, 80, 155, 157, 158, 159, 161
Lincoln, President 9, 144, 165
Littlejohn, John 86
Livingston, Robert 110
Louisiana Purchase 55, 110
Lowell/Francis 100, 101, 137
Lynn 101, 137

M

Madison County 33
Maine 62, 137
Mainline Canal 60, 69, 116, 160
Manchester 101, 137
Manhattan 14, 25, 149, 166
Marbletown 84
Marquette 45
Maryland 46, 60, 62, 128
Massachusetts 20, 53, 67, 100, 101, 125, 128, 165
Memorial Day 10
Merrimack River 101, 137
Miami 131
Middlesex Canal 53, 67, 137
Millwright 96, 97
Minuit, Peter 14
Miracle of Rosendale 90, 91
Mississippi River 62, 97, 103, 113, 120, 124, 132, 140
Mohawk Indians 14
Mohawk River 52, 57
Moosic Mountains 74
Morris Canal 141, 156, 157, 160, 161

N

New Amsterdam 13, 14, 16, 17
Newark 141, 160
New Brunswick 157, 158, 159
Newburgh 67, 69, 70, 152
Newcomen, Thomas 105, 106, 107, 108, 122
New England 26, 28, 45, 62, 79, 80, 88, 101, 103, 104, 109, 113, 115, 129, 134,
    135, 136, 137, 138, 139, 142, 143, 145, 146, 148, 157, 158, 163, 164, 167
New Jersey 14, 48, 60, 65, 67, 69, 80, 101, 103, 111, 113, 139, 140, 141,
    142, 143, 145, 151, 159, 160, 166

New Paltz 5, 20, 21, 84, 85
New York and New Jersey Port Authority 166
New York Central Railroad 162, 166
New York
 (City) 3, 5, 7, 25, 47, 58, 59, 60, 67, 68, 69, 70, 71, 72, 74, 75, 80, 84,
  87, 90, 111, 113, 125, 129, 132, 140, 141, 143-150, 158, 159, 160, 161,
  162, 165, 166
 (State) 3, 4, 6, 14, 17, 20, 23, 27, 28, 33, 36, 41, 47, 48, 56, 57, 58, 60, 63,
  65, 66, 67, 68, 69, 71,72, 76, 80,81,83, 84, 89, 93, 94, 96, 98, 101, 103,
  104, 110, 111, 113, 114, 115, 116, 121, 122, 124, 125, 126, 134, 135, 138,
  139, 141, 142, 143-154, 155, 158, 159, 160, 161, 162, 163, 164
 (Upstate New York) 145, 146, 150, 151, 152, 153, 158, 160, 161, 162
Niagara 24, 25, 58
Nicolls, Colonel 17
Norfolk/Albemarle Canal 62
North Branch Canal 156, 157, 161, 162
Northwest Territories 27, 55

O

Ogden, Colonel 111
Ohio 1, 55, 56, 60, 62, 120, 131, 132, 140
Olyphant, George 81
Oneida 152
Oswego Canal 58, 144

P

Paper mill 98
Passaic 141, 160
Paterson 141, 160
Patroon 15, 16, 19
Pennsylvania 20, 26, 36, 37, 41, 45, 46, 53, 58, 60, 62, 64, 65, 66, 67, 68,
 69, 71, 72, 74, 75, 76, 80, 81, 83, 86, 87, 101, 103, 115, 116, 117, 119,
 125, 128, 129, 139, 140, 145, 146, 155, 158, 160, 161, 162, 163
Pennsylvania Coal Company 81
Philadelphia 4, 8, 46, 47, 60, 64, 65, 66, 68, 71, 80, 110, 116, 125, 131,
 135, 138, 139, 140, 142, 146, 157, 158, 159, 163, 167
Philipse family 25
Phillipsburg 157, 160
Pilgrims 20, 128
Pittsburgh 24, 60, 62, 116, 120, 132, 139, 140
Pontiac, Chief 24
Portage railroad 139
Port Jervis 67, 68, 70

Portland cement 31, 32, 39, 40, 86
Potomac 27, 56, 131
Pottsville 46
Poughkeepsie 69, 152
Pozzuoli 31

Q

Quakers 20, 64, 128
Quartering Act 24

R

Races, Steamboat 113
Rahl, John 9
Railroads 4, 51, 59, 63, 81, 83, 120, 130, 132, 138, 140, 142, 146, 151, 160,
    162, 163
Raritan 62, 141, 156, 157, 158, 159, 160, 161
Raven Rock 158
Rensselaer 15
Revolutionary War 22, 24, 25, 26, 28, 45, 55, 58, 146, 150, 155, 159
Rhode Island 62, 99, 137
Rochester 153
Roebling, John 11, 75
Rome 30, 31, 43, 130
Rome, NY 114, 152
Ro ndout 7, 67, 70, 74, 75, 76, 79, 82, 145, 147
Rondout Creek 5, 7, 8, 9, 11, 19, 21, 36, 70, 87, 88, 93
Rosendale 3, 4, 5-12, 13, 19, 20, 21, 23-29, 30, 33-41, 61, 63, 68, 70, 71,
    76, 77, 78, 80, 82, 83, 84-94, 95, 98, 135, 148, 154, 164, 167
Rusten, Jacob 8, 20, 21, 84

S

Sailing ships 27, 140, 157, 158
Saint Lawrence 23, 101
Salina 57
Savery, John 105, 106, 107
Saw mills 7, 20, 26, 97, 98
Schenectady 150, 151
Schuylkill 60, 65, 66, 68, 76, 155, 157, 159
Scranton 46, 81
Seneca Canal 144
Shawangunk Mountains 25, 67, 69, 70
Sickels, Frederick 121
Slater, Samuel 99, 100

Smearton, John 31
Snyder 11, 25, 136
Statue of Liberty 3, 39, 103, 165
Steam power/engines 4, 102, 105-115, 116-126, 133, 134, 138, 145, 150, 164
Stevens, John 141
Stourbridge Lion 74, 75
Stuyvesant, Peter 16, 17
Surinam 17
Susquehanna 126, 161
Syracuse 57, 58, 152

T

Tanneries 26, 98
Tannersville 153
Tappan Zee 25, 67, 69
Textile Mills 98, 99, 100, 129, 137, 141, 148, 151
Thru-put 60, 69, 155, 1595
Tilson 11, 85
Titusville 140
Tontine Coffee House 47, 48, 71
Treaty of Breda 17
Trenton 157, 158
Trevithick 123
Triangular Trade 18, 136
Troy 47, 150, 151
Truth, Sojourner 8, 9
Tugboat 87, 114
Turnpike 26, 139

U

Ulster County 70, 71, 72, 78, 84
Uncle Sam 151

V

Verranzano, Giovanni 13
Vertical corporation 80, 163
Virginia 46, 56, 62, 131

W

Walkill River 7, 20, 25, 36, 67, 87
Walkill Valley Railroad 7, 9
War of 1812 28, 45, 56, 100, 135, 136
Washington, D.C. 56, 131

Washington, George 8, 56, 131, 152, 159
Water Rights 102, 103
Water Wheel/power 26, 87, 94, 95-104, 109, 125, 138, 145, 150, 157, 164
Watt, James 96, 105, 108, 109, 110, 111, 116, 117, 119, 122, 123
Welland Canal 58
West Point 8, 47, 69, 152
Westchester County 25, 146
White, Canvass 33, 36, 70, 77
Whitney, Eli 100
Wilkes-Barre 46, 81
Williams Lake 5
Windmill 26, 95, 133
Window of Opportunity 159, 162, 163
Woodstock 5
World Trade Center 166
Wright, Benjamin 68
Wurts Brothers: Maurice, John, William, and Charle 64, 65, 66, 67, 68, 71, 72, 75, 76, 78, 79, 80, 81
Wye level 53

Y

Yonkers 25